Teaching, Learning
and
Primary Mathematics

Editor
Adrian Pinel

Teaching, Learning and Primary Mathematics

Contents

Contents

The articles included in this book are from:
MT: Mathematics Teaching, Published by the Association of Teachers of Mathematics

Editor: Adrian Pinel, University College Chichester.

Cover Photograph :   Karen Smith, taken at Scotholme Primary School, Hyson Green, Nottingham

Teaching, Learning and
Primary Mathematics:
Beliefs, Evidence and Challenges

This design is taken from the ATM Activity Pack - Holes
The pack contains 16 full colour cards illustrating holes from the environment,
plus photographs of computer generated images

Holes pack prepared by Lyndon Baker and Ian Harris

Teaching, Learning and Primary Mathematics: Beliefs, Evidence and Challenges

Beliefs

Members of *ATM* have long espoused the belief that learners of mathematics are entitled to teachers who pay considerable attention to *how they learn, how their minds work* and accommodate to this in their teaching. We have expressed the belief that 'human learning always goes beyond what it was given because of the personal contribution of the learner' and have recognised that a consequence is that the learner's own methods are a vital element in their own and others' learning. We have pressed the case for 'big ideas' of mathematics to be communicated through the medium of the curriculum at all its levels, and that the powerful images and patterns of mathematics should be encountered by all learners.

From its start, our association has seen the important ways in which practical materials can be used to mediate and communicate ideas. We have held firm to the central place of problems - their solving and their posing - within the discussions between learners and teachers that animate learning and bring classrooms to life. In summary, this collection of articles resonates with a positive reaffirmation of a belief in young children as powerful learners of mathematics.

Evidence

Beliefs are not enough in today's world, and the evidence to support them that appears in the pages of *Mathematics Teaching* is essential if we are to sustain a principled stand when we are buffeted by politically motivated actions and meet less informed or enlightened viewpoints - for though it is a cliche, it remains true enough that 'everyone knows how we should teach because they once went to school'.

Evidence from well-founded substantial research is vital, as are the vibrant glimpses of classroom action that give us pause to reflect and consider how children learn, and how we teach. *MT* often contains both kinds of evidence; the research is not presented in the stylised format, but in a straightforward way that conveys key findings and challenges. As it is now becoming more widely accepted in this country that changes and practices should be grounded on well researched evidence, *MT's* mediating role is vital in helping our culture to change. Perhaps, one day, we will find our curriculum far less tossed or turned by political imperatives and its own design deficiencies, and instead based upon a balanced spectrum of evidence from research and classrooms.

GENERAL INTRODUCTION

Adrian Pinel

Challenges

Meanwhile, we are faced with immediate challenges in primary mathematics. In meeting them we must remain aware that they will pass away - in just a few years time the national numeracy strategy and related numeracy projects will have been left behind us, replaced no doubt by newer urgencies.

The *Numeracy Task Force's* numeracy strategy will promote changes in practice that will inevitably include some aspects that we would wish to endorse - for example, more emphasis on mental calculation and the development of a confidence in, and feel for, number, combined with the delaying of written methods. At the same time we pay a price for any new orthodoxy as some are constrained to move away from effective methods and approaches to conform. Equally, there is already considerable misconception about the strategy and it will inevitably be subjected to widely varying interpretations - I know of one school who have used it to justify short quickfire mental *tests* each day and the teaching of standard algorithms *earlier* than before!

This is a far cry from providing the scaffolding of experiences that help children to build their mental strategies and mental images of number; on this basis, building a range of jotting and other written methods, that they can use flexibly because they understand why and how they work, having exposed them to discussion and testing; or acquiring facts by figuring them out and through recognising patterns; or using engaging ways of practising that help facts to become more readily available.

Each challenge is also an opportunity to build a more enduring legacy: greater understanding of mathematics as a network of ideas, facts, strategic questioning and reasoning, and of the implications this has for learning and teaching. It brings awareness of connections to centre stage: firstly, within mathematics this, for example, makes a nonsense of a curriculum so dominated by numbers that geometrical ideas are neglected; secondly, between mathematics and various contexts, where a real awareness of each context can give life to mathematics, and vice-versa. As teachers, we need to recognise these and teach so that learners come to own them too, and so are able authentically to use and apply their mathematics.

Section 1:
Using and Applying Mathematics

This design is created using one of the hexagon designs from the ATM Tiling Generators series of Tiles.

How many tiles does the smallest closed shape need?

How many circles does each pattern contain?

Tiles designed by Robert Ives

SECTION 1:
Using and Applying Mathematics

One of the great and successful movements in mathematics education has been the increased emphasis on 'using and applying' since the Cockcroft report: 'Mathematics Counts' in 1982. It was industry and commerce in the 1970's who called for schools to send out young people *not just* with the academic knowledge of mathematics but who could *also* use and apply that mathematics, able to show flexibility within a rapidly changing workplace environment. *Using and Applying Mathematics* was formally made a significant part of the National Curriculum in 1989, and since then, despite many attempts to sideline or remove it, has been consistently re-asserted. The central tenet is that there is little point in acquiring necessary knowledge or practising skills if the learner then does not have a sufficient understanding of how and when to use these. The successful application of knowledge and skills in fresh contexts is not only a clear indication of depth of understanding, but also vital if learning is not to be bound by the narrow or abstract contexts in which it is acquired.

Within this area lies the seeds of the movement for mathematics in primary schools to find a place within the wider curriculum, rather than as an isolated subject. The problem solving nature of mathematical thinking had long been recognised as developed within

mathematics itself, then used and applied throughout the curriculum. The increased emphasis on problem posing led to more young learners developing and refining their natural ability to be questioning, thinking mathematizers. At the heart of these movements was always the vision of the mathematics classroom as one not just of activity but of communication: "discussion between pupils and teachers and between pupils themselves" (Mathematics Counts §243.)

Quite correctly it was exceedingly difficult to separate out selections for this section, since there is a lot of the spirit of *Using and Applying Mathematics* in the rest of this book. However, 'Better Mathematics' (1987) found that changes in classroom practices are only sustained where there have also been changes in teachers' perceptions and beliefs. Research into this area is provided by the first article: Alison Millett and Mike Askew's "Teachers' Perceptions of Using and Applying Mathematics" (1994) in which they summarise findings across all of the key issues from a two-year NCC-funded research project.

Bill Rawson's article: "Authentic Activity in Learning Primary Mathematics" (1992) offers a positive reaffirmation of a belief in young children as powerful learners of mathematics; drawing from an LEA teaching and learning Project, it centres on the idea of 'authentic activity' with the primary classroom as a place where mathematical meanings and concepts are negotiated, and where learners 'learn to use (mathematical) tools as practitioners use them'.

The learners' viewpoints are revealed in "Children's Impressions of Mathematics" by Tony Cotton (1991) who was inspired by a conference discussion group to enquire into younger primary children's perceptions. His final five questions challenge us still.

There are three shorter contributions, each of which illuminates an aspect of Using and Applying Mathematics in primary contexts.

The importance of discussion is revealed delightfully in Jeanette Harrison's contribution to "Young Children Talking about Mathematics" (1993), as is the vital place of manipulatives in providing an image to provoke that discussion.

Suzanne Peterson's "Linking Mathematics and Science in the Primary School" (1994) shows how some mathematical skills can find a place to be developed and practised within Science contexts.

Finally, Andrew Bramwell - "Transferring Approaches Between Subjects" (1993) compares approaches to English and mathematics lessons, raising some key questions that still seem remarkably topical - shades of plenaries?

Alison Millett and **Mike Askew** worked on the Evaluation of the implementation of National Curriculum Mathematics at key stages 1, 2 and 3, a two-year research project funded by the National Curriculum Council.

TEACHERS' PERCEPTIONS OF USING AND APPLYING MATHEMATICS

"Yes, I try and make it relevant to them and their lifestyle ... things like shopping lists, or adding and dividing and making averages, rounding up and approximating and things like that. I think if you can't relate it to life, they don't get the meaning of it."

(Year 5 teacher)

"... they had to measure a variety of parts of the body and record the answers."

(Year 2 teacher)

"Well you know ... how many children are here, how many are away, that sort of thing ... if... so and so wants to go to the painting table, and we can only have four on, if two have gone already, how many more can go, that sort of thing."

(Reception teacher)

"Yes, I would say that that is where you really look at the using and applying mathematics ... outside the maths lesson... although ... before they can apply it they've got to use it, and that 20% of the time is within the maths lesson ... using . . . the applying tends to come in other subjects."

(Year 6 teacher)

If these interpretations of using and applying mathematics fit with your own, then the work of the NCC Maths Evaluation Project [1] would suggest that you probably share them with many other teachers. On the other hand, you may find these interpretations limited, perhaps because they are not in tune with ideas expressed in the Non-Statutory Guidance, and may be tempted to regard these interpretations in terms of a deficit model of the intentions behind this attainment target (Mal). But thinking in terms of

such a deficit model may be an unproductive way of viewing teachers' implementation of Mal.

This article attempts to make the case for closer scrutiny of the reasons behind interpretations made by teachers - and primary teachers in particular - and to suggest positive ways forward.

Initial reactions to Mal

The inclusion of ATs 1 and 9 (now Mal) in the NCC 1989 Mathematics Order produced a variety of responses. For some teachers, including many readers of this journal, the development of 'using and applying mathematics' as a necessary and valued part of the mathematics curriculum was long overdue; they did not need to be convinced of its value; indeed, they were practising a problem-solving approach in their own classrooms and were familiar with the aims of all aspects of these two attainment targets.

For many other teachers, however, reactions were different. They had viewed the mathematics curriculum in terms mainly of content, and the idea of process skills, which were supposed to 'stretch across and permeate all other work in mathematics' (Non-Statutory Guidance p.D1) was new to them. They were familiar with most of the mathematics National Curriculum, with a few obvious exceptions in the areas of probability and algebra, but their familiarity did not extend to the language of communication and reasoning, logic and proof required by ATs 1 and 9.

The mandatory nature of all parts of the curriculum meant that teachers could not ignore these attainment targets, but had to try to address the unfamiliar issues as best they could. Evidence collected by both the National Curriculum Council [2] and Her Majesty's Inspectorate [3], indicated that teachers were having difficulty in interpreting the statements of attainment of ATs 1 and 9 in a way which enabled them to identify progression.

The NCC Maths Evaluation Project

The NCC Maths Evaluation Project began its work in 1991. One of the aims of this two-year evaluation of the implementation of the mathematics National Curriculum at key stages 1, 2 and 3 was to investigate the difficulties for teachers that had been noted, even at that stage, in the implementation of ATs 1 and 9 (as they then were), and to identify promising practice in this area.

The project was funded by the National Curriculum Council and involved the collaboration of researchers from King's College London (Centre for Educational Studies), the University of Birmingham School of Education, and the University of Cambridge Institute of Education. Data collection was by questionnaire survey (to 1100 teachers in 11 LEAs with a 68% response rate); in-depth interview (with 32 teachers at key stages 1, 2 and 3); through case studies in a small set of schools; and through the work of two teacher groups meeting together monthly during the two years of the project. Each of these data sources informed, to a different degree, the work of part of the project which was focusing on 'Using and applying mathematics', but the primary data sources for this were the questionnaires, the interviews and the case studies. Teachers were asked in interview to describe some work in their classrooms which they considered to be related to ATs 1 and 9 (the interviews were conducted before the second Mathematics Order became statutory), and to discuss how typical this was of the way in which they approached this part of the mathematics curriculum. They were also asked about their views of the relationship between ATs 1 and 9 and other attainment targets, and about

progression within 'Using and applying mathematics' itself.

Early findings of the project indicated a discrepancy between teachers' perceptions of the extent of implementation of Ma1 and the HMI and NCC findings of limited take-up.

Analysis of the questionnaire data suggested that, particularly at key stage 1 and key stage 2, the majority of respondents did not regard coverage of 'Using and applying mathematics' as particularly problematic, although a substantial proportion of teachers did indicate that they perceived difficulties in the implementation of Ma1. These difficulties included: a lack of teaching experience in Ma1; inadequate coverage by commercial schemes; lack of clarity in the meaning of SoAs and programmes of study; difficulty in classroom management and organisation for Ma1 at key stage 1 and key stage 3; and difficulties related to the need for changes in teaching style. Questionnaire data also revealed that few teachers used the Non-Statutory Guidance frequently or rated it highly for planning purposes.

A consideration of the interview data gave some indication of possible reasons for the discrepancy between teachers' perceptions and HMI and NCC findings on take-up of ATs 1 and 9; there appeared to be wide variations in teachers' interpretations of this attainment target, with many teachers making interpretations which fitted with their current practice. The nature of some of these interpretations is illustrated by examples from interview data.

The use of practical work

The use of practical work as a means of implementing Ma1 was frequently mentioned by teachers interviewed. Whereas some practical activities, like baking cakes, apply the use of measures, many of the examples discussed by teachers in interview had more of a sense of starting with a piece of mathematical content and then finding some means of making it practical by embodying it either within physical materials or diagrams, or within some sort of 'real-world' context. Examples of 'practical as embodiment' included measuring body parts, using pebbles for sorting, drawing fraction 'cakes'. This key stage 1 teacher, asked whether she could recall an example of a recent activity, which involved the children in using and applying their mathematics, replied:

"Um, not recently, but off the top of my head, they had to measure a variety of parts of their body and record the answers. They were given a tape measure... and asked for circumferences round their head and foot sizes and shoes and they just had to go away and record their answers."

(Year 2 teacher)

Many of the teachers describing such an interpretation of practical work reported high percentages of time spent on using and applying.

The use of everyday classroom contexts

Teachers also described using everyday classroom situations as contexts for mathematics, and indicated that they viewed this as using and applying mathematics. On her questionnaire, this reception teacher had put that more than 80% of her mathematics time involved using and applying. In interview she elaborated on this:

"Using maths in everything, yes. I mean we have a brick, a plastic brick for each child and I divide the whole class into four teams ... so each child has got a plastic brick and they're in four colour sets and then when somebody is away we put the plastic brick on the side, so we've got a very visual, very large scale representation of who's here and who isn't."

The need to make mathematics 'relevant'

Alongside an emphasis on practical work, teachers also spoke of the need to make mathematics 'relevant'. There seemed to be an underlying assumption that as long

as real objects were used, children would find the activity relevant. For many teachers, particularly at key stages 1 and 2, relevance appeared to come about through a focus on everyday applications like money; measurement in its various forms and day-to-day numeracy.

"They're using number work in the shop, when they're adding up the prices. I mean, I gave them little shopping bills that they had to give to another person, so they're actually doing number work there. Simple addition and subtraction not realising that they are doing it, six take away six or whatever, but they are actually using their number work."

(Year 2 teacher)

Interviewer: *"Can you give me an example of something they've done (involving using and applying)?"*
Teacher: *"Oh, things like shopping lists or adding and dividing and making averages, rounding up and approximating things like that, I think if you can't relate it to life they don't get the meaning of it. (Later) I think its just that I try and make it relevant, and try and make it so that they can see what's happening to them, maybe away from school at home."*

(Year 5 teacher)

Application of mathematics in other subject areas

The application of mathematics in other subject areas was also believed to satisfy the requirements of the target.

"..... we did quite a lot of art work out of symmetry, that was quite good ... again the art work came from the maths, but I suppose it doesn't really matter ... we used and applied the maths that we'd learnt in the classroom to do the art work ... which was quite nice."

(Year 5 teacher)

Implications of these interpretations of 'Using and applying mathematics'

Taken together, the interpretations described above could span much of Mal, but teachers appeared to favour particular aspects rather than a balance between several aspects. It was rare for a range of examples to be offered by one teacher in an interview.

Some teachers interviewed for the NCC Maths Evaluation Project, having made their own interpretations of Mal, felt satisfied that they were implementing Mal, and felt in consequence that much of the mathematics in their classrooms involved Mal. Other teachers perceived that Mal was new to their teaching, and required them to change their practice.

Where teachers were able to question their own practices and beliefs, marked changes could be precipitated. This key stage 1 teacher described how previously she had presented mathematical topics in 'little units' aimed largely at individuals, but the challenges presented by Mal and its associated assessment had brought about changes:

"Talking in groups more, over things, and letting them come up with their own ideas and then letting them carry on, and then setting things up which they can ... I would do the tasks and set them at different levels to start it, (now) it's finding tasks that they can work within levels ... (Later) I'm not there but at least I know where I'm supposed to be going."

(Year 2 teacher)

A Year 3 teacher described standing back more:

"... so I might just ask leading questions of that child, and hope to nudge them on to understanding a bit more."

For other teachers the requirements of Mal did not fit comfortably with their beliefs and caused anxiety and confusion.

Interviewer: *"Yes, and when you're planning, do you actually look at attainment targets one and nine, to put those into your plans?"*
Teacher: *"Well I look at them, I do look at them and each time I look at them I think ... well I really ought to include these, and I come up against this sort of feeling that*

... they don't work. (Later) Well, actually I felt that I was doing a lot better before attainment targets one and nine came along, because, I would always try and relate whatever topic was being done, like number work or something, back to a practical outcome, ... like shopping lists were a favourite of mine and, I don't know, paying for things and working how many of so much out and somehow this is lost in attainment targets one and nine. I mean maybe it's just my perception of it but somehow I don't feel that what they've put in there has any particular relevance to real life."

(Year 5 teacher)

In some cases the interpretation made of 'Using and applying mathematics' seemed to have led to the belief, expressed by several interview teachers, that little specific planning was necessary for this attainment target.

Interviewer: *"Do you actually put it into your plans at the moment, ATs 1 and 9?"*
Teacher: *"It's a good question, I have to be honest, I mean, ... I probably don't directly, no ... I think I tend to hope that I cover it on the way."*

(Year 5 teacher)

Some parts of the attainment target appeared to have received more attention than others. When teachers were asked to describe the pupil behaviours, which they were trying to encourage, there were indications that teachers were not providing opportunities for all three strands of Mal (applications, mathematical communication and reasoning, logic and proof). At key stages 1 and 2 teachers were more familiar with providing for the potential to use and apply the techniques, but not the strategies of mathematical problem solving and justification. The communications strand was also not frequently mentioned.

When talking about differences in pupils' abilities in Ma 1, teachers often described these in terms of pupils' personal qualities, particularly confidence. Pupils identified as more able in 'Using and applying mathematics' were largely described in terms which were not directly to do with their mathematical ability, but with their being prepared to think about things, seeking out the teacher if stuck, having had lots of experience outside school and generally being able to transfer ideas. Perhaps as a consequence of this focus on personal qualities, teachers did not appear to see the need to teach the strategies of 'Using and applying mathematics'.

Discussion

The variations in interpretation of Mal, and consequently in its implementation, revealed by the work of this project, indicate the complexity of implementation for many teachers. Teachers may never have considered the issues raised by Mal in their mathematics teaching, and the resources, which they had been using for years, did not, in the main, raise the issues for them. Many primary teachers, feeling that their strengths did not lie with mathematics, have relied almost exclusively on published commercial schemes as mediators of the mathematics curriculum.

If teachers had found these commercial schemes successful in the past, there was no reason to suppose that this reliance would change with the introduction of the National Curriculum, particularly at a time for primary teachers when so many other subjects were demanding their attention. However, commercial schemes did not (with some exceptions) help teachers greatly with ATs 1 and 9, and although efforts have been made by publishers since the first Mathematics Order was produced to incorporate work related to what is now termed Mal with the introduction of the new Order, these efforts have tended to be in the form of either 'bolt-on' activities, or claims of invoking Mal by 'real-life' contexts. Such efforts may be more the result of constraints on publishers than lack of vision. Publishers have experienced serious difficulties in planning for future publications when alterations have been made to the curriculum with little concern for lead times for new materials, and the provision of these materials has unavoidably lagged behind for them.

Nobody's mathematical planning has been helped by first a National Curriculum in 1989, followed by a second version in 1991 and now the prospect of yet another revision being prepared by working groups in 1994.

Without a great deal of assistance from their most familiar source of support, teachers had to rely on their own interpretation of the document in implementing ATs 1 and 9. Even a cursory glance at the programmes of study and statements of attainment from the 1989 National Curriculum (at the levels appropriate to key stage 1) would indicate that teachers' interpretations of Mal may well have been limited by the document itself. It may be that the actual wording of the attainment target itself did not present clearly enough the intentions expressed in the Non-Statutory Guidance. A focus on level 1, for example, of old AT1, would indicate that if children were 'using materials for a practical task' (PoS Level 1), they would be engaged in work which involved 'Using and applying mathematics'. Almost every activity in a key stage 1 classroom could be considered to fall into this category.

It is noticeable that the examples given in the 1991 mathematics National Curriculum differ in kind from those given in the 1989 version, those in the later document making it plainer that the mathematics should be identified as an integral part of an activity which requires its use for successful completion. 'Use measuring in cooking' (example, level 1, 1991) is different in kind from 'compare objects to find which is the longest, tallest, etc.' (example, level 1, 1989), which most teachers would describe as part of the teaching of the measurement of length and would always have included in their teaching of this topic. The change in teaching approach (identified by some teachers as required for the proper implementation of Mal), may well not have been identified by the majority of teachers, and the additional curriculum guidance materials in which this change in approach is spelled out more clearly (Mathematics programmes of study -

INSET for key stages 1 and 2, and 3 and 4, [4]; Using and applying mathematics books A and B [5] have not reached all schools.

It may also be that the unfamiliarity of the content of ATs 1 and 9 (now Ma 1) led some teachers to focus initially on what they saw as the appropriate level for their class, thus establishing little idea of what progression in this attainment target would entail in terms of provision of experiences for pupils. (There were some indications from the project that this happened initially in the unfamiliar area of probability, but that this situation was more easily remedied than for Ma 1.)

In number, for example, few teachers would think in these terms, as their familiarity with this area of mathematics means that they have a progression 'in their heads' and therefore have a longer view of the attainment target, taking into account the different attainment levels of their pupils. In all early years classrooms, teachers are creating environments of which numeracy is an integral part, because they are aware of the sorts of activities that will help their pupils to become numerate. The creation of an atmosphere where problem identification and solving is encouraged, where children's own methods are communicated to others and respected by teachers, where the idea that mathematics consists of only right or wrong answers is given no credence, may not yet be seen by the majority of teachers as an essential precursor to pupils development through the strands of Ma1.

The stranding poster that accompanied the 1991 mathematics document presents the progression through each strand much more clearly. As teachers become more familiar with the higher levels of this attainment target, it may be that the sort of approach needed to develop children's skills of reasoning, logic and proof, and their ability to communicate their mathematics becomes more explicit, and the development of these skills may become part of the mathematics planned for children at earlier stages in their school life.

The results of the NCC Maths Evaluation Project indicate that teachers have made initial interpretations of Ma1, and many of these do not fit with the expectations for this attainment target as set out in the Non-Statutory Guidance. It has been suggested that this is not surprising considering the nature of the National Curriculum itself, the limited take-up of the Non-Statutory Guidance, as revealed by this project, and the limited time which teachers have had to reflect on their interpretations in the light of experience. Ofsted, reporting in 1993 on this part of the mathematics curriculum found a modest growth in emphasis from previous weak development, with the assessment of Ma1 still causing difficulty to teachers in all key stages [6].

The results of the NCC Evaluation point to the need to build on and extend the differing interpretations that teachers may hold of Ma1, and to challenge and develop these interpretations. The results were based on a limited number of interviews, and these interviews took place in the first half of 1992, and so there may be changes already in teachers' interpretations. The teachers interviewed answered certain specific questions. It may be that other questions now need to be asked to promote re-examination and reflection on this important aspect of mathematics. It may also be that teachers and schools from all key stages should work together to design appropriate forms of INSET to help teachers to interpret the Order in a way which permeates all their mathematics teaching.

The current situation should be considered in the light of teachers' increasing familiarity with the 1991 National Curriculum, so that INSET may be appropriately targeted at those parts of the attainment target which teachers can identify as being absent from their repertoire at the moment, and therefore perhaps the most difficult to integrate into their practice. It is to be hoped also that those responsible for revising the mathematics National Curriculum will take the opportunity to clarify and exemplify the intentions behind this important part of the mathematics curriculum.

References

1. M Askew, M L Brown, D C Johnson, A Millett, S Prestage & A Walsh (1993) *Evaluation of the Implementation of National Curriculum mathematics*. London: School Curriculum and Assessment Authority.
2. NCC (1991a). *Report on monitoring the implementation of the National Curriculum core subjects 1989-90*. York: NCC.
3. HMI (1991) *Mathematics key stages 1, 2 and 3. A report by HM Inspectorate on the first year 1989-90*. London: HMSO
4. NCC (1991b). Mathematics programmes of study: INSET for key stages 1 & 2. and INSET for key stages 3 & 4. York: NCC.
5. NCC (1992). *Using and applying mathematics, Books A & B*. York:NCC.
6. Ofsted (1993) *Mathematics key stages 1, 2 & 3: Third Year 1991-1992*. A report from the office of Her Majesty's Chief Inspector of Schools. London: HMSO.

Mike Askew works at the Centre for Educational Studies, King's College, London and Alison Millett is now a full-time research student there.

It is not easy to apply mathematics authentically within the classroom. **Bill Rawson** describes some collaborative work with infant teachers who were making effective use of the interests children brought into their classrooms.

AUTHENTIC ACTIVITY IN LEARNING PRIMARY MATHEMATICS

As a participant in a teaching and learning project with teachers from Devon LEA, I have had the opportunity to collect accounts of numerous classroom events concerning mathematics from around the county. One particular group of teachers with whom I work is attracted to the notion of 'authentic activity'. We encountered this term in an article by Seely-Brown, Collins and Duguid [1] who suggest that, since mathematical concepts are the product of negotiation between mathematicians, students come to understand mathematics only if they 'learn to use tools as practitioners use them'.

Children are quite capable of deciding what they will learn and how they will learn it. Our intention is to work with this notion of authentic activity, to enable students to use mathematical tools, and to identify events which enable students to act meaningfully and purposefully.

A short period of time had been set aside for children in a reception class to share their books. In spite of the fact that the choice of books was entirely in the hands of the children, a 'turtle sticker' scrap book was not exactly what the class teacher had in mind, However, she encouraged her class to continue with their sharing.

There is nothing exceptional about providing children with opportunities to share books. It happens in hundreds of classrooms round the country. What is of interest, however, is the outcome of this particular event. Two cultures, those of the classroom and of the child, had intersected on this occasion, and the children's imaginations were captured by the current craze for turtles.

The tightly knit group of turtle-sticker swappers brought to life what initially appeared to be a mundane activity. By standing back and observing this group engrossed in their work, the class teacher realised they were handling numbers far beyond her expectation. Questions such as 'Do you have a 1, 7, 3?' together with the activities of matching numbers to cards and sorting them into family groups provided evidence of worthwhile engagement with the activity.

This classroom snapshot shows mathematics as an event. The mathematics which was used was not divorced from the lives of these children. It was embedded in the problems the children encountered as they formulated and carried out their plans. To the children, this was an authentic activity. The teacher used this event judiciously. It provided her with sufficient evidence of the children's understanding of mathematics for her to prepare further activities to challenge each child in that group. The children's attempts at working with the number system had provided her with a baseline from which she could work. This group of children were immersed in and confronted by intellectual challenges far beyond counting up to 10.

Sharing events like the one described is a natural outcome of a project conceived as a partnership between Devon LEA and its teachers and the University of Exeter and its tutors. The project focuses on the quality of children's learning experiences. Partnership is reflected in all aspects of planning, monitoring, teaching and evaluation, which are the responsibility of a managing group of teachers, advisers and tutors. The first year of the programme involved 120 participants, formed into local groups. Each group consisted of around ten teachers, guided by other teachers acting as facilitators.

The facilitators, working alongside members of the University staff, supported and promoted the work of the participants. Four one-day conferences, spread throughout the year and held at the University, brought all the members of the project together and afforded opportunities for sharing and for further planning. Each participant was expected to focus on a specific issue in connection with the core subjects; this needed to be an issue which was recognised as a concern for their particular school. Their school-based work in connection with the project was required to enhance children's learning at key stage 1.

The planning of work which gives children experiences of high quality has been approached from many different angles as a result of asking the following five questions:

- **analyse -**   *'Where am I now?'*

- **set aspirations -**

    'Where do I want to go?'

- **plan and enact -** *'What must I do?'*

- **evaluate -**   *'How did I get on?'*

- **disseminate -**

    'How can I share what I did?'

Among those involved with the project, the value of well-organised and direct forms of didactic instruction was not disputed. What interested teachers was the search for other kinds of teaching which would help them reconsider their planning and raise their awareness of how children are learning as well as what they are learning.

The teacher who recounted the turtle event considered mathematics to be a language - a communication system used to explore and expand our knowledge of the world. With this in mind, a model of

mathematical literacy can be drawn out of the event. The children's knowledge was situated and purposeful. It was situated within the current ambient culture for those children, which was their interest in turtles. The children's involvement with turtles was interpreted by other teacher participants as a mathematical experience. Whenever children engage in mathematical experiences there is a potential for them to learn mathematics, to learn about mathematics and to learn through mathematics. Teachers suggested that learning mathematics means learning how to use mathematics and is, therefore, the result of activity within situations where children have particular purposes and intentions. Mathematical literacy means moving beyond familiarity with number symbols to include, as in the turtle account, an understanding of the ideas and processes that the symbols represent. Through this authentic activity, children are drawn into experimentation with how the number system works and operates. Activity, concept and culture are interdependent. Consequently, mathematics is viewed as an integral part of personal and social needs. This view of knowledge acquisition implies learning through mathematics. Valuing knowledge acquired within a socially accepted context has important implications for our understanding of knowledge of academic subjects and of how classroom experience might be managed in order to help children acquire such knowledge. It is this search for evidence of learning in mathematics that has led participants into trying to identify authentic activities within the school life itself. The following example might help to explain what participants felt were 'authentic activities'.

Each morning, a time is set aside for the reception class teacher to 'take the register'. Children sit in a circle and it is normal practice for the teacher to provide number challenges for children to work on while the register is called. A teacher with a large registration book on her lap must present quite an imposing sight for young children, especially as the response made by children are followed by the teacher drawing marks down the columns that divide each page. After one such period of registration the teacher realised the child on her left had also taken the register and wanted to check with her teacher that their 'numbers' tallied.

Here is an example of a process that was modelled quite unintentionally by the teacher, and yet became a powerful tool by means of which a child could explore properties of number. This child was applying a technique for learning which she had applied frequently during her pre-school years. Her understanding of the function of this regular circle time led her to imitate the process carried out by her teacher. This was not mere mimicry. The child modelled her behaviour on that of the teacher, because she appreciated the purpose of this daily ritual - counting is important because it tells you 'how many': how many places to set for dinner; how many will sit at a table; how many will be going home today; how many shelves will be needed to store the lunch boxes... Is it because she realised the significance of this ritual that she wished to check her results against those of the teacher?

Authentic activities have purpose, are coherent and are meaningful. They are the ordinary practices of our culture. Seely-Brown, Collins and Duguid [1] alert their readers' attention to the danger of distancing classroom tasks from the activities of authentic practitioners.
They write:

"School activity too often tends to be hybrid, implicitly framed by one culture, but explicitly attributed to another. Classroom activity very much takes place within the culture of schools, although it is attributed to the culture of readers, writers, mathematicians, historians, economists, geographers, and so forth. Many of the activities students undertake are simply not the activities of practitioners and would not make sense or be endorsed by the cultures to which they are attributed. This hybrid activity, furthermore, limits student's access to the important structur-ing and supporting cues that arise from the context."

For this reason, participants welcome

AT1, in which using and applying mathematics is put forward as a way of viewing and making sense of the real world.

They are encouraged by the reminder within the Non-Statutory Guidance of the National Curriculum Council that mathematics is not a series of disconnected, abstract ideas. They also value attempts to provide opportunities for children to explore mathematical ideas in context, by working through thematic approaches. To help achieve this, participants in the Partnership project attempt to identify authentic activities within the school culture.

Authentic activities in mathematics allow children to solve their problems in a variety of ways. When children control the strategies for problem solving, they can adapt both the problem itself and also the strategies they apply to it. Authenticity occurs when there is a perceived personal need. This highlights the importance of using a variety of approaches, to ensure that an activity is entered into by children.

In the following account Petrie Murchison invites us into her classroom:

Thomas (4.11) came to me and said:
"I want to make an Advent Calendar.
Will you help me?"
Me: *"What do you want your Advent Calendar to look like?"*
Thomas: *"A house one."*
Me: *"What do you think you will need to make it? Shall I make a list for you, then we can go and get the things you need?"*
Thomas: *"Cardboard, felt pens, masking tape."*

I wrote a list. After fetching what he needed, Thomas worked at cutting out his shape. He wanted some help with making it stand up so I gave him some technical help attaching 'sides' cut out by him so the house would stand up.

Thomas numbered the first two doors '1' and '24'. He knew that 24 was Christmas

Eve. I felt he had an idea of the numbers that lay in between but was unsure of the enormity (for him) of the task that lay ahead. He wrote numbers randomly to start with and kept asking me to write them. All this happened on Friday afternoon. When he returned to the task on Monday morning, he got down to his work immediately and wrote all the numbers himself.

Thomas: *"I'm up to two and oh."*
Me: *"That's twenty. You don't have many more to do now. You've already done number twenty-four. Do you know how many more you need?"*
Thomas: (Counting and holding up fingers) *"21, 22, 23, 24. I need three more."* (Elatedly)

A few minutes later...

Thomas: *"Look Miss. I've finished. There are no pictures under it."*
Me: *"That's the next thing, Thomas. What are you going to draw?"*
Thomas: *"Christmas Trees."*

A little while later...

Thomas: *"Oh, look. I've done number six gingerbread man too tall and too wide."*
Me: *"Don't worry Thomas. You could put another little door on to cover him up - like a stable door."*

What follows in Petrie's account seems to sum up all that is good in the Partnership project - the opportunity to share our perceived successes, doubts and pitfalls in order to enhance children's learning.

'Bill, I jumped in again, I think I acted spontaneously because Thomas was anxious about what he had done at this stage. I felt he needed reassurance. Again this piece of self-initiated work has endorsed my thinking about children's development in mathematical thinking:

- They often work with larger numbers than I had anticipated.
- They are in control of their own learning.
- They are able to work on a sustained task.
- They show persistence and self-motivation.
- They demonstrate their spatial awareness and use appropriate vocabulary

... and probably more!'

Bill Rawson works in the School of Education at the University of Exeter.

References

1. J Seely Brown, A Collins and P Duguid, 'Situated cognition and the culture of learning', *Educational Researcher*, Jan-Feb 1989.

Following a discussion at the BCME Conference in 1991 **Tony Cotton** decided to ask children what they think mathematics is

CHILDREN'S IMPRESSIONS OF MATHEMATICS

At the BCME Conference 1991 I was a member of the discussion group which was set up to explore ways in which the culture of mathematics, whatever that might be, and the culture of the mathematics classroom affect the child in her perception of mathematics and therefore her learning of mathematics.

The discussion focused on the clash between the view of mathematics as a pure science and the view of mathematics education as a social science, the latter acknowledging the affects of the cultural context of the school within which mathematics is learned.

In order to start looking at the way culture can influence children's learning we decided to discuss the issues with the learners themselves. Three members of the group agreed to begin some initial research with three different groups of learners; a group of mixed ability early learners, a group of high-achieving school leavers, and a group of low-achieving school leavers. This is an initial report or the mixed-ability group of early learners.

Some of my questions were:

- How do children perceive mathematics?
- Do they have preferred ways of learning?
- Do out-of-school educational experiences affect this?
- Is the image of mathematics affected by the age of the child?
- Is there any link between children's background and their image of mathematics and its learning?

These were my own starting points and, though I did not expect to answer any of

these questions during the project, I hoped to become clearer about which questions might be important to ask.

How we describe children's background is a crucial and complicated question. How can we define children's background without immediately falling back on our own stereotypes? Allowing children to define their background for themselves seems to be a sensitive and sensible approach. It is also vital that children realise that it is acceptable and desirable to use their experiences out of school to understand and develop the work they do in school.

The project

I worked with small groups of children throughout the school across the age range 5 to 9, starting with the first-year infants and working up through the age range. The groups contained about six children and as nearly as possible reflected the ethnic and gender mix within the classes, which were mixed-ability.

I wanted to use the same starting points for all children and I also wanted to try and link the activities I would be using with the activities the rest of the class would be doing. To this end I settled on four mathematical activities with a common thread of change, to fit in with the whole-school theme.

Together with an introductory session and a review, this would form a six-week block with me working with the children for half a day a week. I had no fixed activity for most weeks, but rather a key question or questions which I hoped the children would respond to in their own way. For some sessions I had a selection of activities which I thought might be appropriate.

The project followed this pattern:

- Week 1: Introduction - What is Mathematics? What is learning? Where do we learn?
- Week 2: Activity 1 - How do people change as they get older?
- Week 3: Activity 2 - How can we change pictures?
- Week 4: Activity 3 - How can we change shapes and patterns?
- Week 5: Activity 4 - How can we change numbers?
- Week 6: Review - What have we learnt?

Throughout the sessions I encouraged children to talk and reflect on what they were learning and asked them to think about ways of recording this.

Children's responses

What is Mathematics?

For the first-year infants, mathematics was not a word which really meant anything. There were, however, lots of interesting comments in the discussion which followed my getting some mathematical equipment (a calculator, some Multilink, various measuring and drawing devices, etc.) out of a carrier bag.

> *"Mathematics - that's to do with adds isn't it?"*

> *"Calculators - my mum uses one of those for shopping."*

When I produced a ruler I was told that they are used for drawing straight lines for writing on, with no mention at all of measuring. During our discussions children used vocabulary such as: spiral, compasses, die and dice and the difference between them, semi-circle, ruler. They very much enjoyed using the compasses and the calculators, although one boy said:

> *"I'm clever, I don't need to use a calculator."*

Using the calculators led to some very interesting conversations such as:

"How do you spell 15?"

The children saw the numbers as words and recognised them as a whole, not as separate digits. There was a lot of confusion between letters and numbers, one child wanted to make the calculator write my name and suddenly said:

"Oh, but they aren't like a,b,c."

This seemed to suggest that children can recognise and use large numbers before they have the understanding of the place value of the digits - numbers can be read before the value is understood.

They also started to find patterns on the calculators and made familiar numbers like phone numbers. We noticed things, such as that all the phone numbers had the same number of digits and all began with 66.

Some of the 7-year-olds were beginning to get ideas about the meaning of maths. One girl said:

"I don't do maths, I do adds."

Another thought it was something to do with times tables. When given a choice between doing some of their own maths or using the maths materials, some did sums of their own and others used the equipment to draw shape pictures. Again calculators were very much linked to their mothers and shopping. This time the children started to notice the divisions on the ruler, although they still told me that it was for drawing straight lines.

The older children saw mathematics as nothing more than number and found it either easy or hard depending on their aptitude with number manipulation. When I asked them to do a piece of mathematics of their own they all instantly got to work on times tables, covering their work so that no-one else could see it. It seemed that mathematics is something we do on our own and cover up so that no one can copy. We made a rule that all our mathematics had to be done in such a way that everyone could see what everyone else was doing.

Mathematics was also associated mainly with businesses such as shops and banks and was something that the children thought men did at work rather than women. However, when it came to describing relations who were good at maths it was again mainly mums, aunties, sisters and female cousins who were talked about.

Where Do We Learn?

The most popular place to learn for the youngest children was at home. Here they learnt to write their names, how to draw, Gujerati numbers, ABC and lots of other things. Most of this learning was from their mothers although all relatives were important: uncles, aunties, and grandmothers. One of the children said he learnt a lot at his dad's work. Other places where they learnt things were the park where they learnt to climb and the swimming baths where they learnt to swim. There was no mention of school. When I suggested school might be a place where we learn things I was corrected quite sternly,

"No, school is where we do our work."

The 7-year-olds decided that there were things you learnt out of school, like reading and letters, and work you did in school like maths. Places other than the home were mentioned as sources of learning - The Mosque, Sunday School and books were mentioned as places or things we learn from. One of the traveller children in the group told us at length about the lorries and trucks they used to tow the fairground rides, and was amazed when this was accepted naturally by the whole group as a good and exciting place to learn. From then he often told us about the fairground and used it to inspire much of his work.

The older children responded in a similar way, although some had tutors at home and talked about Saturday School as a new place of learning. There was still a difference between the learning out of school - learning to make things, learning Gujerati, learning reading and writing - and

the doing in school - doing maths, doing spelling and so on.

Learning was still a word that the children felt uneasy with. They thought work was a better word for describing what goes on in school, particularly anything seen as mathematical.

How do people change as they get older?

The first-year infants decided people got bigger and fatter as they got older. They decided that the best way to show this was to draw round a selection of people. They used brothers and sisters in the school, themselves and me to show the difference in shape with age. They didn't think you stopped growing and in their recording showed people who were 500 years old and very big indeed. They didn't measure in any way, feeling that the pictures spoke for themselves.

There was a very similar response from the seven-year-olds. However, when I asked them about how we might examine this they didn't want to come up with any ideas of their own. They felt more comfortable being told how to do it. They also found it quite difficult to work on one outcome as a group, preferring individual work and worrying about copying. They finally chose to work in two groups, one of boys and one of girls.

With the junior class we adapted this activity slightly and made scale models of pondlife we had found the previous week on a pond-dipping session. We used these models to illustrate the life cycles of frogs and mayflies. Although it took a long while for the children to realise that I wanted them to make decisions for themselves and that I wasn't going to feed them the methods, they created some brilliant moving models.

In an excellent reflection session the children decided on three headings to describe their learning process:

- ***things that we learnt*** - these were things they didn't really understand before the activity but understood now;

- ***things we had to work out*** - these were tactics they employed to help them move forward in the process;
- ***things we had to do*** - these were skills they already had that they used during the investigation;

I give the list below. It seems to me to be an excellent way to examine the process of learning after an activity. It also started to suggest to me what I mean by a child understanding a particular skill. I think children understand something when they recognise that they have used that skill effectively.

We learnt:
About the animals in the pond. How the animals change during their lives. To try things out first and then make them better.

We worked out:
How many pieces we needed in the models. How many fasteners we needed to make the models. How to measure the animals to make sure they were the right ones.

We had to:
Cut out carefully, count, measure, estimate and write.

Changing Pictures

The 5- and 6-year-olds enjoyed making giant pictures by enlarging using different-sized squares, but didn't explore using other types of grids. They were however very competent at this enlargement exercise which many teachers in other schools have told me are too difficult for young children. This was one of their favourite activities. Our discussion at the beginning started to frustrate the seven-year-olds:

"When are we going to get on with our work? When are you going to tell us what to do?"

They were beginning to get better at listening to each other. They were also starting to learn that rushing through tasks just to finish them is not always fulfilling. Sometimes involvement in, and exploration of mathematics can be a

motivation in itself.

The enlargement grids worked very well on all sorts of levels, from practice in colouring carefully, through lots of language of shape, to an early discussion of scale factor with one of the older groups. There was a general awareness of the number of squares in the grids and the location of these squares. We also started to investigate areas and think about describing position using co-ordinates.

Changing Triangles

The youngest children enjoyed making pictures out of triangles. One decided you can make anything out of triangles. We had interesting discussions about what colours we should use to make sure all the connecting triangles in a square were different colours, and how many colours we would need. Making a collage using their triangle pictures proved to be a good activity to encourage group-work as we all worked on one large picture. They even noticed that if you put two triangles the 'same' next to each other you could make a square and that a triangle was 'half a square'.

The seven-year-olds also began to notice all sorts of details about pattern and shape. The outcomes ranged from one child spending a long time colouring very carefully keeping in the lines, something he hadn't done previously, to a girl who was starting to think about fractions.

The oldest group I worked with exhibited a clear grasp of fractions, and doubling and halving to guess how many of the triangles would fit into each other. We decided to make a puzzle book for the rest of the class which proved a great motivator for finding more and more facts about the triangles. One of the boys who had great difficulty in recording things had the most well-refined mental methods, describing the way to work out how many triangles would fit into each other depending on the number of halvings which had taken place. This was far beyond what would have been 'expected' of him in a more formal context.

Changing Numbers

The youngest children used the calculators to make big numbers. They recorded their favourites which were either patterns they found interesting such as 19191919 or really big numbers. One boy stopped using the calculator to make big numbers as he couldn't fit enough numbers on the display, thus showing an understanding of place value. A couple of the children used the constant function to generate sequences. Another just used the calculator as a counting aid, first putting 1 on the display, then cancelling it and putting up 2 and so on. One child refused to have anything to do with it as he 'couldn't do numbers'. This was the same child who had refused to use a calculator in the introductory lesson as he was clever and didn't need to.

The seven-year-olds found it harder to explore numbers with their calculators; they wanted to do proper sums and then check the answers. There was much less discussion about the nature of number than among the younger children.

Again, the older juniors were a bit wary of using calculators to do maths with. They saw them mainly as things you use after you have done some maths to check if it is right. One child decided to list as many ways as possible of making 80. He told me it could be 100 take 20, or 4 twenties, or 75 add 5 and lots more. I was impressed, and suggested making a list and using the calculator to find other ways. He started this and then looked confused and asked me:

"What do these mean?"

pointing to the + and - symbols on the calculator. It struck me how much mathematical knowledge and ability many children have, but never show because they are unsure of how to describe what they have discovered.
As John Holt says in *What do I do Monday?* [1],

"What we can do, ..., is to help children find our labels for the ideas they have already grasped."

What have we learnt?

At the beginning of each session we reflected on what we had done in the previous week and what the children felt they had learnt. The infants quickly became used to the idea of recording the activities in some way and by the end of the six weeks were making very sophisticated comments about their learning. They felt less comfortable about setting their own targets, usually preferring to rely on me for suggestions.

The older children found any discussion of previous work difficult and put a great deal of pressure on me to tell them what this week's 'work' was rather than talk about last week's work. When I asked one girl to explain some work she said,

"Oh why is there always a because? It just does it."

They found describing what they thought they had learnt from the activities difficult to explain, usually just outlining the mechanics of the task. I think learning to describe the ways you have thought through a problem is particularly difficult. Whenever I work with teachers and ask them to describe their thought processes there is often a prevalence of language such as 'thingys' and 'whatsits'. We need to allow children to develop mathematical language to aid them to think mathematically and therefore develop mathematically.

Despite this all the groups were positive about the project in general. Even those children who informed me at the beginning of the sessions that they were no good at maths or that they thought maths was boring!

Conclusions

I don't think it would be appropriate to attempt to conclude anything from a relatively short period of time in this school, and so my conclusions are in the form of questions which have been raised in my mind during the project:

- Why do children see learning as something which happens at home or other places and work as something which we do in school?

- Why is reading and writing something children see as learning and mathematics something children see as work?

- Mothers are obviously seen by children as one of their most important teachers. How can schools acknowledge and take advantage of this?

- Children come to school with a wealth of mathematical knowledge and experience. How can schools build on this?

- Children seem to think that teachers have all the questions and answers. How do we encourage children to start asking their own questions and exploring their own answers?

References

1. John Holt, *What do I do Monday?*, Unwin, 1970

Tony Cotton is a mathematics consultant who lives in Leicestershire

In MT144, three teachers, **Jeanette Harrison**, Jane Scown and Vin Marshall each described working with young children, focusing on their mathematical language. This is Jeanette's piece.

YOUNG CHILDREN TALKING ABOUT MATHEMATICS

Zero means nothing

Whilst being aware of the importance of encouraging children to both discuss their mathematical ideas and to verbalise their understanding, I was rather concerned that there somehow never seemed to be the time or opportunities to develop these strategies in my Y2/Y1 classroom.

I felt that my main problem was an organisational one. Whilst trying to make the majority of maths tasks set interesting and challenging I found that I was creating situations in which an overwhelming number of children required my attention. This obviously prevented me from spending any valuable amounts of time with any of them.

Therefore, before I could consider my interaction with the children, my priority was to think about my organisation. Helen Williams (maths advisory teacher) was due to spend some INSET time in my classroom and it was decided that we would look at organisation with an underlying awareness of interaction and discussion.

For a morning session we decided to use three activities which needed varying amounts of teacher attention:

- ATM pattern tiles: to be explored on the carpet. This for the main would need little attention (although at the end of a session their patterns would be discussed).

- A calculator and 100 square activity: this would require periodic visits.

- A calculator and multilink activity: this, we felt would require most of our time and provided the following observation.

The children had been introduced to the calculators earlier in the week and had 'explored' and 'recorded' anything they considered worth remembering. Since we had also spent a lot of time on patterns that term it seemed quite natural that they showed patterns on their calculators. Some had also recorded phone numbers, the 'maths date', sums and repeating and growing patterns.

Helen asked the children to look at these previous records and see if they could show on their calculators what they had recorded. When they had done that successfully they were asked to 'make it' in multilink. There were various responses. One particular Y1, Abbie, had reproduced her phone number which was 40112. It was displayed on her calculator, and she made the following model.

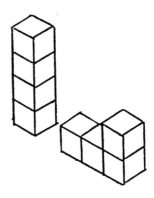

She was asked to repeat it (a term she had been introduced to previously). This she did, firstly on her calculator (11240112). Oh dear, it didn't fit. So she repeated her multilink pattern *(see below)*.

Ben, who was opposite, had begun to take an interest in Abbie's phone number. Helen asked him if he could see what it was. He queried why she had left a space and wanted her to stick it all together, (like everyone else's!)

Abbie explained that the space was for the zero; but Ben was obviously not very happy about that. At that point I almost jumped in with an explanation, but instead asked Abbie if she would like to explain a little bit more to Ben.

"It's for the zero" she said again, but was now beginning to doubt herself.

Ben went on to say that she needed a cube there for the zero, (he wanted it represented!), but she argued back that her phone number isn't 41112, which is what it would look like if she put a cube there.

He still looked unsure. Abbie answered,

"But zero means nothing, so I've put nothing there".
Yes, he understood this.
"I understand" he said.

Jeanette Harrison is Maths Co-ordinator at Threemilestone Primary School, Truro.

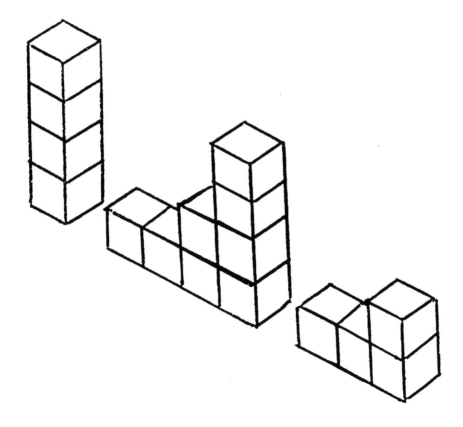

What is a slater? How far does it walk? **Suzanne Peterson** explains.

LINKING MATHEMATICS AND SCIENCE IN THE PRIMARY SCHOOL

Connecting maths and science allows for dual outcomes and generates needs and purpose on the part of the learner, which leads to understandings and skills practised in a meaningful way. Neither the maths nor the science are trivialised. It is not a case of trying to teach two things at once and possibly failing at both but rather generating one skill from another through an authentic link.

Two approaches

There are two approaches to integrating maths and science that have proved to be effective. The first way begins with a science investigation and extracts the pertinent maths skills from the activity. This allows for a planned coherence in the science concept development but no hierarchy of mathematical concepts and skills: even so, the requisite maths does arise naturally and has meaning and validity for the children. For example, in a series of activities about how the body works, an experiment to find individual lung capacity using containers, water, plastic tubing and deep breathing led to the need to measure volume with some accuracy, to decide on an appropriate unit, to understand the property being measured and to estimate, compare, check and record.

In the second approach the science springboard can also enable a teacher to introduce a prepared, concomitant mathematical skill. For example, activities about shadows in the playground involve not only watching the movement of the sun, but also measurement of length, awareness and recording of time, and could include consideration of the changing area of shade cover or lead to projective geometry.

Network of concepts and skills

A network of concepts and skills can be developed in accordance with children's interests and needs. Care needs to be taken that the programme is driven by concepts, not by activities which means that the planning and direction of integrated lessons need to be carefully thought out. The ideas of measurement and fair testing should underlie explorations and tasks.

Taking a problem posing approach creates opportunities for investigations that often appear to be either scientific or mathematical but in fact make use of combinations and the natural linking of several ideas. Packaging an animal shaped biscuit (we have ten centimetre teddy shaped biscuits available in Victoria) and posting it through the mail requires consideration of structures, possibilities in transit time, cost, visual representation of findings, to say nothing of the high personal involvement in the safe voyages of the teddy.

This approach helps promote autonomous learning behaviours characterised by choosing, persisting, and achieving a solution that has been independently determined by the learner.

When I began a unit on 'cold blooded creatures' I defined the maths skills that I though would be required for the science activities: I found that the skill the children actually required or practised was quite different. I set objectives leaving room for the children to pose problems, design investigations and extend their findings. Generally the children's ideas were more interesting than mine and small groups of children would work at different tasks within the stipulated topic. My objectives included observing, inferring, asking questions, considering variables, fair testing and measuring, as well as the consideration of values, but the tasks themselves were developed by the children.

The mathematics that arose from any particular investigation followed no designated cognitive hierarchy. When a child needed to know how to do something the skill was introduced and used immediately. It was left to the teacher to follow up the mathematics at another time with reference to the original task.

This was very productive, because children took responsibility for their own acquisition of skills, which they were likely to master by using the new information to reach a goal. I monitored and recorded all the maths concepts and skills that arose, so that they could be revisited and reinforced in more formal or varied ways.

What do ants like?

A group of five- and six-year-olds were finding out about small creatures in the garden. On one occasion we had brought some ants and spoonfuls of nest dirt into the classroom. The first thing to discuss was what we already knew about ants. There was a general consensus that ants always went to sweet things. Always! The group was adamant: they had seen them on honey jars and spilled cordial. I wanted the children to test this belief. We negotiated a task which included setting up a tin tray with a spoonful of sugar solution at one end and a spoonful of nest dirt at the other. A lone ant was put into the centre of the tray. We watched for three minutes. We found out something about one ant, so we replicated the investigation with different ants on different trays. We had similar results. Were beliefs about to change?

We then put a drop of solution near the nest outside and made another series of observations - and so another investigation began. But the maths?

Watching our original ant scurrying around the tray (keep a paintbrush on hand for the gentle push back), running to and fro, required some counting. I heard a five-year-old counting every time the ant ran to the solution,

1, 2, 3, 4, 5, 6, 7, 8, 9, 10...
1, 2, 3, 4, 5, 6, 7, 8, 9, 10...

Her companion was trying to write down each figure as it was called. Another child had drawn up two columns, 'to the sugar' and 'to the nest', and was diligently tallying. We talked about making a gate of five. Afterwards we practised this with clapping and tapping. We used calculators and did a five count watching the numerals go by, saying them aloud and noting any patterns; we recorded fives with the traditional hand prints.

A body of skills

A body of maths skills soon accrues. A teacher keeping records of activities and skills will notice gaps in the content and ideas arising in science which need revisiting and extending. The conventional boundaries of skills should not be seen as an impediment: the teacher follows and supports. The child learns and the teacher learns from the child. A six-year-old boy had been studying garden slugs. He wanted to draw a big slug that was exactly like a slug. The child was not accustomed to centimetres so he used paper clips as his unit. The tiger slug was three paper clips long and half a paper clip wide on its mantle. The black stripes were about two paper clips long. So make the length nine paper clips: for every paper clip of the real length put down three for the drawing. The stripes he found would be six paper clips long. He had some difficulty with the half paper clip but was helped to a result. He was delighted with his drawing and its precision.

Once the science is planned and an informed overview of possible concepts considered, the teacher has only to be alert and flexible. The maths programme for the following weeks can spring from one simple task. Here is an example and a description from my experience.

Slaters

Slaters (sometimes known as pill lice or wood lice) were under observation. The question arose: how far does a slater walk in five minutes? The activity could be organised as follows:

1. Make a paper tray. (A3 paper is suitable). Using a paint brush put a slater on the tray. Set the timer for five minutes. Put your pencil just behind the slater and follow his path, do not push him! If he pauses put an X on the spot. After five minutes return the slater to its habitat.

How will you measure how far it walked?

Many different ideas were tried. Someone used wool and the group decided that this was a good idea. The length of wool equivalent to a slater walk can be measured against a known unit. Winding it around a thirty centimetre ruler is manageable although a child pointed out that there was extra wood at each end of the ruler so the count ought to be by thirty-one. The children enjoyed this new counting by thirty ones and noticed a pattern and checked earlier estimates. The science lesson can continue according to your science aims but the maths can be pursued in the following ways.

2. Make different trays with A3 paper. How many different ones can be made, with and without cutting? Do all the trays hold the same volume of centicubes or sand? Talk about volume and the different units that can be used.

3. Work on patterns in counting. What happened to the numerals in the thirty one count? Pairs of children can work on making different patterns using the calculator or the star pattern on a number 'clock'. A nine-year-old found that if you add up two consecutive even numbers the sum is double the odd number in between the two evens. He trialled this extensively and was satisfied with his discovery.

4. Discuss a useful unit for measuring a slater walk. What is a centimetre and a millimetre? Who else uses them? Where did they come from? Find something else as long as your slater's walk, or twice as long or half as long. How many slater walks between the classroom and the gate?

5. Devise with the children some number problems about walking long distances. An eight-year-old asked, "If you know that a slater is one centimetre long and it walks 190 centimetres in five minutes, how far would I get if I walked at the same rate?" and "If I am x centimetres tall I'd have to walk how many centimetres?" He did not have an answer himself but his group members refined the question and worked it out.

6. The slater was followed for five minutes. Can the children estimate five minutes? Estimate and check how many words can be read in five minutes, or how many names written. These are not unusual mathematics activities but the child's previous experience gives them meaning and a recognisable point of reference. A week's interesting maths unfolds before your eyes!

Suzanne Peterson teaches at Deakin University in Victoria, Australia

MT abounds with 'short-bits' and 'snippets' of writing between the longer articles. In MT139, **Andrew Bramwell** compared his approaches to English and mathematics.

TRANSFERRING APPROACHES BETWEEN SUBJECTS

As with most primary teachers I employ a variety of strategies for working with individuals, groups and classes of children. The approach used is adapted according to subject. However, one aspect of teaching which I have found to be essential, and easily overlooked, is the role spoken language has to play in the development of mathematical thinking.

The NC document recognises this point in AT1 where children are required to talk about tasks being undertaken e.g. *talking about their own work and asking questions* (Maths 1, level 1) or *explaining work and recording findings systematically* (Maths 1, level 3). The acquisition of this skill cannot be assumed to be a by-product of the mathematics curriculum; it is a vital component of learning and has to be planned for in the same way as work on shape or number.

Comparing approaches

As a teacher I find it interesting to compare approaches adopted during an English lesson to those of mathematics. Firstly, a teacher will try to hear the children read as often as possible. During this session there may well be questions designed to assess the level of comprehension. These questions may be literal or inferential:

• *What do you think will happen next?*
is a common means of encouraging the child to predict possibilities in a logical and imaginative way.

• *Can you tell me what the story is mainly about?*
requires the individual to summarise and look for the main ideas.

• *What would happen if ...?*
where often a key element is changed so that new unforeseen developments have to be constructed.

These are important steps on the road to understanding and using the English language; steps which need to be built upon in order to gain insight, and most importantly confidence, in discussing and questioning material placed before them.

The same is true of mathematics. Situations need to be created where children can explain, question and communicate their discoveries to a variety of audiences. These may range from a working partner, to an ability group, the class or on an individual basis with the teacher.

One method I have used in order to increase the amount of mathematical discussion is to borrow an idea from our Early Years Unit where *High Scope* is followed. I introduced a *recall* session: at the end of each lesson a small number of children were invited to recall certain elements of work and are given the opportunity to explain how they approached individual tasks; to verbalise their thoughts sequentially e.g. first I did this, then . . .Other children are invited to ask questions, the rule being that the questions should be fair and considered. In this way the whole class are involved, gaining confidence not only in the use of mathematical vocabulary but also in the formation of meaningful questions. The recall session might only last five minutes, but it is a five minutes well spent, not least for the teacher who is in a position to make judgements about the children's understanding.

I have recently taken the idea a step further by introducing a planning session at the beginning of each lesson, or group of lessons; again this was an idea borrowed from *High Scope*. Children have to plan their approach to a particular topic. It is at the planning stage that objectives are clarified so that the children are aware of what they are actually aiming for. This may sound complex, but in reality may be quite simple:

- *During this lesson I would like you to practice multiplication of HTU by U, and think of a real life problem to ask the class in recall where this type of multiplication sum has to be used.*

If the comparison is made with prediction exercises in English a good deal of discussion can be drawn out, for example, when algebra is under investigation:

- *Can you see a pattern?*
- *How can this pattern be continued?*
- *What would happen if...?*
- *How could the pattern be changed?*

I find it important that children's confidence is built up; they should not be 'put on the spot' but encouraged to think about and question material placed before them.

Look carefully at this:

$$463 - 212 = 675$$

Is this answer correct?
Why?

How was the answer worked out?
Invent other 'incorrect' questions for others to look at.

When I use planning and recall periods I suppose I am hoping that children are given the opportunity:

- to explain their decisions
- to consider the implications of those decisions
- to be willing to accept suggestions not only from the teacher but also from their peers.

As confidence grows it is possible to see a more discerning approach to mathematics, even from those children who have real difficulties with the subject. During *recall* it is possible to discuss the relevance of mathematics to the real world; to see shape and number at play in the environment and to refer to other curriculum areas.

Do you remember when we talked about structures in technology?

What did we learn?
How did mathematics help us?
How can technology help us to solve this mathematics problem?

Recall time should not become a simple question and answer session, but a time to exchange ideas and thoughts between all those involved; a time when children are encouraged to put their thoughts into words.

Andrew Bramwell teaches at Collingwood Primary School, Great Barr

Section 2:
Numbers, Calculating
and Calculators

This design is taken from the ATM Activity Pack - Spirals
The pack contains 6 full colour photographs showing where spirals are found
in the real world, along with computer drawn spirals.

Spirals pack prepared by Lyndon Baker and Ian Harris

SECTION 2:
Numbers, Calculating and Calculators

Background influences

It is always a surprise just how long it takes for ideas to move from being originated, trialled, and established by wider research and enquiry, to the point where they are in commonplace use in the classroom. The *'ATM Numeracy Project'* has worked with patience and understanding over many years to bring these ideas to fruition.

In *'Notes on Mathematics for Children'* ATM members reasserted the primary place of numbers in mathematics, while at the same time rejecting those who would "put the clock back". This influential book focusses on language and experiences, how numbers can be transformed, their properties, and on variety in ways of calculating.

One of the founders of ATM, Caleb Gattegno, developed innovative and successful methods for teaching young children about numbers and their relationships, many of which are behind the contributions here.

Development work signalled as needed by the Cockcroft Report: *'Mathematics Counts'* in 1982 led eventually to the most substantial and widespread primary mathematics project this country has so far experienced, and to which ATM members contributed strongly: the Primary Initiatives in Mathematics Education Project (PrIME); with its offshoot project The Calculator-Aware Number Curriculum Project (CAN) the PrIME Project helped to bring forward positive and effective approaches.

The articles

With a CAN background, Sue Gifford contributes a challenging article showing that young children can become active makers and negotiators of symbols. Building on the work of Martin Hughes and others, her enquiries reveal how some 6 & 7 year olds chose to represent number operations.

Janet Duffin, as an evaluator for the CAN project, reveals graphically through examples of children's recordings, and analytically, how interdependent mental calculation and calculator work are in developing children's ideas about number. Her view echoes that of CAN that calculators have something special to contribute to learning about numbers.

Alan Wigley's radical re-appraisal of the teaching of number draws upon and interprets Gattegno's work; it calls into question many of the common practices of primary classrooms, offering alternative prescriptions. Eddie Gray and Demetra Pitta also focus on symbols as they reveal the case of an 8 year old, Emily, whose understanding was enhanced substantially by the introduction of a 'supercalculator' along with a programme of study based on exploring combinations of numbers and operations with a common result.

Where the latter two approaches emphasise abstract structure, Meindert Beishuizen's focus is also on children's strategies and how they 'see' numbers.

The 'empty number line' not only enables children to develop strategies that support their mental calculation, but also provides us with a graphic insight into those strategies. This, and other key images of numbers, are bound to be a growing factor in our teaching of number.

Kevin Holloway's description of a project carried out by a group of primary teachers reveals one way in which ideas about the teaching of number can acquire a firm place in the classroom. When teachers 'see it happen' for themselves and can discuss their observations with others, they come to believe in the learning benefits. Interestingly, Kevin questions whether the *National Numeracy Project* will be able to deal effectively with the links between mental strategies and their written versions and 'standard' written methods.

Finally, Mike Askew returns to the distinction made elsewhere between *knowing* and *figuring out* within mental calculation and the dynamic relationship between these. His analyses of expectations at key stages 1 and 2 are sure to act as a useful checklist.

Sue Gifford considers how younger children use number symbols.

YOUNG CHILDREN'S REPRESENTATIONS OF NUMBER OPERATIONS

When do children start to use symbols to represent practical addition and subtraction situations?

This was the question that arose from the work of Martin Hughes in 1986. He had found that not one of 90 'sum-fed' infants chose to use plus or minus signs to record practical addition and subtraction activities.

With the help of colleagues from the ILEA Abbey Wood Maths Centre, and from the ILEA CAN project, I have collected various examples of children's own arithmetical recording, including invented symbols. They point to the ingenuity of some children when faced with the problem of representing number operations.

Being involved in working with six year-olds and calculators (as part of the CAN project in ILEA), I wondered if the introduction of the calculator would help to make children more likely to use the standard symbols to record practical activities.

I chose to do the 'yoghurt pots' activity with pairs of six year olds. Each pair had a pot with six nuts: one child had to turn over the pot, leaving some nuts out, and trapping a number under the pot for the other child to 'guess'. When they had become confident in doing this, I gave the children paper and pens and questioned them:

Could you put something on paper to show all the different ways that you've found?

I assured them that they could show this any way they liked. Initially they were unsure. Eventually they all set to work,

except one child who did nothing at all, insisting he could not think of any way of recording the activity.

The rest of the group's results are shown here. The children had used a variety of ways of recording, including pictorial, written and symbolic, but none had used conventional symbols. I then realised that I was unclear how to assess or interpret the children's representations.

Of the two children who chose a written mode of recording, Ashley produced a string of letters in a 'whole sentence' format, writing across the page, and apart from using numerals, using the conventions of written language. He read his work as,

'I can make two in and four out. I can make three in and three out.'

John, in contrast was more economical and read his work as:

'three in and three out, four in and two out, six in none out, one in and five are out.'

This seemed to indicate a move towards abstraction in the elimination of superfluous words and so I judged this to be a more 'mathematical' piece of recording.

Then I looked at Thu Hein's work: she had chosen a pictorial mode for her recording. Far from abstracting key mathematical information, she had included minute details of the nuts, using the conventions of close observational drawing (encouraged by the school art policy at the time). I concluded that she may have been more interested in the nuts than my imposed request! I also realised that her perception of the task may have been quite different from mine: how was she to know why I wanted her to record? Not having any real purpose, how was she to decide that a simplified mathematical mode rather than an elaborate artistic one was called for? Perhaps she had done her best drawing to entertain me, or for me to put on the wall and show parents and visitors.

On the other hand, Thu Hien's work was arranged in a highly mathematical tabular form: there were in effect two columns of paired drawings showing the numbers of nuts in and out of the pot (and showing almost all the possible combinations, with no duplicates). I suddenly realised that, instead of a series of equations, such as 2 + 4 = 6, *which I had in mind*, she had used the most effective layout for recording number combinations. Hers was a pictorial version of a list of number pairs.

In one way, then, Thu Hien's work was an effective mathematical representation, without being at all symbolic. (But then, by asking the children to record number *combinations*, I had presented no real need to represent any *operations*, symbolically or otherwise. Something which I had overlooked.) Was this evidence, in NC terms, of being able to 'record things systematically' AT1 level 3?

Jancev was the other child who had used a pictorial mode to record, and she had used simplified drawings of the nuts, together with numbers. 'This seemed more mathematical, as redundant detail of nuts and pots had been omitted and helpful numbers added. Despite this apparent sophistication, Jancev's record is hard to comprehend. The pictures are dotted about all over the page. Although the pictures on the left, 4 and 2, or 3 and 3, may be intended as pairs, it is not possible to work out her intentions from the others. The need for pairing, or spatial organisation of some kind, is evident.

One child did attempt to use symbols. Katie arranged numerals in a vertical column, alternating them with lines. She read her page as follows:

'plus two, plus four, plus five and one, two and four.'

This seemed to show that the lines were intended as plus signs. What struck me about this was that although Katie does not know the plus sign and how to use it, she does know something about the conventions of written arithmetic, namely the vertical format. The fact is that you can combine numerals with signs which are called things like 'plus'. Exceptionally, what she did, unlike all the children in Hughes sample, is recognise an arithmetical activity and attempt to use the appropriate written conventions. The reason for this possibly lay in my role as a maths consultant, known to the children as someone who regularly came to do maths with them. My presence no doubt signalled to Katie that this was a maths activity. Hughes' presence with the children he studied would not carry the same influence. And yet he had used obviously mathematical language like 'add' and 'take away' which could well have given some children a clue. Katie's readiness to use symbols is therefore not totally explained: perhaps her experience with the calculator (slight at this stage) or the novelty of writing arithmetic had produced positive attitudes?

Later I did the same activity with a group of six and seven year olds, who were more arithmetically confident and so had ten counters in their yoghurt pots. To my surprise and delight, Susan asked if they could have paper to keep their scores, thereby supplying the children with their own purpose for recording. I subverted this by suggesting that they also make a note of the numbers of counters involved.

None of these children used whole sentences or pictures, and all used a vertical list format. Typically, Steven used numerals and the words, 'in' and 'out' for maximum brevity. Sarah improved on this by grouping the 'ins' and 'outs' together, and so using a listed pairs format. Then I spotted Susan, who was recording the activity by writing standard equations. So much for total irrelevance of the operations symbols or of the equation format to this activity!

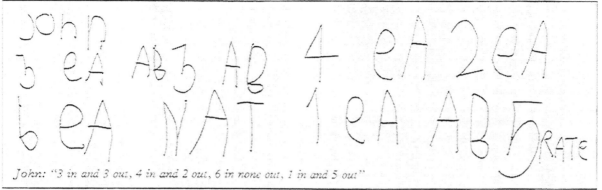

Ashley: "I can make 2 in 4 out. I can make 3 in 3 out."

John: "3 in and 3 out, 4 in and 2 out, 6 in none out, 1 in and 5 out"

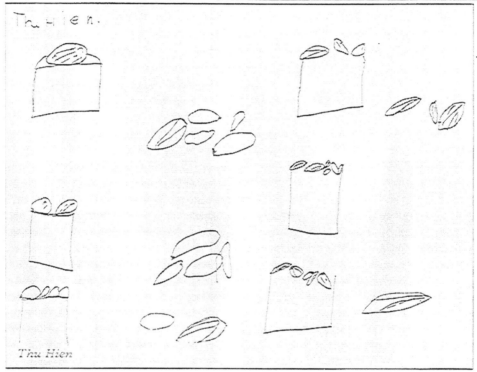

Thu Hien

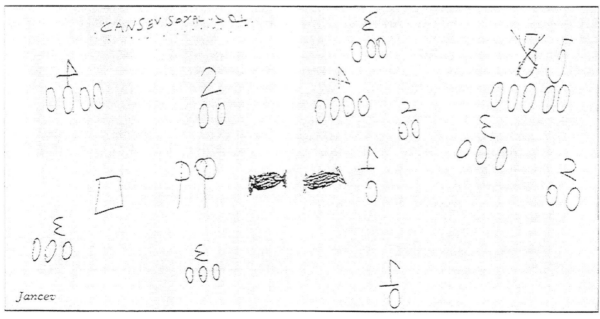

Jancev

Interestingly, Susan had come from another school where she had done formal arithmetic. It seemed that she knew and understood the conventional way of recording number bonds, and had identified this as a 'number bonds' activity. Presumably as with Katie, she had been able to read the contextual clues (e.g. my presence) so as to select the appropriate format from her repertoire.

What happened next was intriguing: Sarah looked across at Susan's paper and copied Susan's last equation, $5 + 5 = 10$. She then wrote at the top of her paper, $2 + 2 = 4$. I presumed that she must have been thinking something like,

'Oh yes, it's one of those, like 2 + 2 = 4.'

Perhaps she was attracted by the standard 'grown up' style, or perhaps she liked copying Susan. Was this a link with her experience with the calculator, or another example of the fact that not all learning is acquired in school? Certainly Sarah was intrigued enough to make connections with her past experience.

In contrast to Hughes' findings, at least two or three children out of twelve were willing to use symbols to record a practical maths activity. It is hard to say why: the calculators may have had something to do with it, perhaps more through creating positive attitudes out of novelty than through any great depth of understanding of the concepts.

One question remained: *when would the rest of the children use plus and minus signs to represent the actual operations of adding and subtracting?*
A practical 'function machine' box was suggested by a colleague, Val Heal. The children have to guess the machine's function from the number of cubes going into and coming out of the box. The value of this activity lay in the focus on the operation being performed, the clear purpose for recording, a defined audience in the writing of instructions for the machine operator, and a need for brevity forced by the size of the paper and the impatience of the children waiting to guess.

Initially, the children's instructions concerned the total number of cubes to be pushed out, rather than the number to be added or taken away. This difficulty in focusing on the operation rather than the total was what Hughes had also found.
(I had assumed that a diet of sums had lead to this, as sums usually require children to work out the total, rather than the operation. However these children were not used to sums, so I presume that operations are hard for six year olds to think about.)

The children then began to write statements like, 'three more' or 'put two', which they subsequently reduced to just '3m' and 'p2', thus using letters as symbols for the operations. Some children began using the equals sign, which they read as 'more' or 'plus'.
(They had frequently referred to the equals key on the calculator as 'plus', perhaps because the equals key is frequently the one that produces the action, and so is more memorable.)
Then one child altered the equals to plus, and after that plus and minus signs became common on the slips of paper. The signs were in various positions in relation to the numbers, to the left, right, or above.

None of the children spontaneously saw the relevance of operations signs to this activity. With encouragement to think of 'quicker ways', however, they went through the process of 'successive shorthanding'. This is described by the Open University's course, *Developing Mathematical Thinking* as the result of an approach which requires children to record activities in their own way, and by repetition of the same activity, to develop more economical forms in successive stages. Certainly the repetition of the activity gives the children time to see the redundancy of some information, to search for abbreviations, and to see the relevance of symbols, either their own, or standard forms.

Their use of symbols may have been related to experience with the calculator, or the similarity of the machine to it. As before, the children had no doubt that this was maths. Perhaps it was that in this

Katie.

*Katie: "plus 2 plus 4
plus 5 and :
2 and 4"*

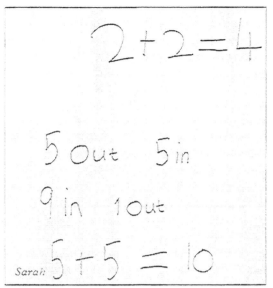

$2+2=4$

5 out 5 in

9 in 1 out

Sarah $5+5=10$

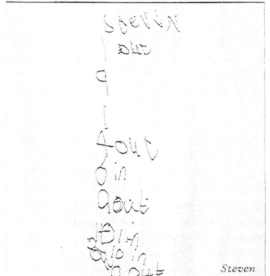

Steven

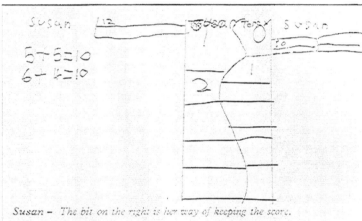

Susan

$5+5=10$
$6+4=10$

Susan – The bit on the right is her way of keeping the score.

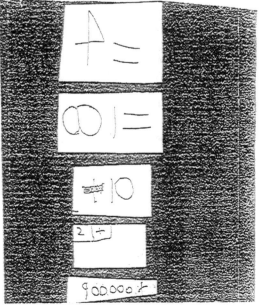

Function machine instructions

activity, as Hughes puts it, 'symbolism serves a meaningful purpose'? Interestingly, they made no attempt to draw. Is this because, as Dufour Janvier and others point out, language is better for capturing actions, while pictures are fine for amounts?

It seems that children as young as five can find ways of representing operations. One interesting activity suggested by Hughes, which provides a meaningful context for symbols, is that of leaving a message to show how many counters have been secretly added to or removed from a box. If the others in the group know the original number in the box, the message helps them to work out how many there are in the box. Whereas Hughes suggested this as a way of introducing plus and minus symbols, Christine Pugh used it to suggest that children find their own ways of writing such messages. Jamie, aged five, devised a system for showing addition and subtraction, without the use of symbols. He simply drew the pot, with the counters taken away shown at a distance, or the counters added shown in the pot. This record is very economical and within the familiar context, needs little or no explanation.

Another interesting example is that of Asif, who did not so much invent symbols, as invent his own number sentence form. He was finding numbers that could be made with any combination of twos and fives, using colourfactor rods, and his teacher, Razia Begum, encouraged him to record his results in his own way with the purpose of discussing them with his teacher and classmates later. He simply wrote down all the numbers used, then ' + ' then the total. He told me that he had written:

'Two, two, plus, four'.

When I asked him what 'plus' meant, He explained, 'Two numbers put together,' (implying that the plus sign showed what you had to do with the whole list of numbers). He clearly understood his invented system, which was far more economical than the standard number sentence, and quite appropriate for the

context. The one drawback of this system is that it does not distinguish between a single digit and a multiple digit number. However the spacing indicates this, and within the context, little confusion is likely to arise. This made me realise that a plus sign may be used by children as a separator rather than as an operator: that is, it performs a punctuation function rather than representing an abstract relationship.

Other children have tackled the problem of separating numbers in their own ways of recording and have got round it in a variety of ways. Sophie used a vertical list, under the heading of the total. Another child wrote, 'two fours makes eight' leaving a gap between numbers, as one does between words when writing and thereby making the multiplication sign redundant. Another child wrote, '11.2 is 22', which he read as, 'eleven twos is twenty two'. Was the dot an invented symbol for multiplication, or merely keeping the numbers apart? This use of mathematical symbols to aid the layout of information underlines the lack of relevance of the operations signs to many contexts. One situation which seems to give rise to the invention of symbols, is that of finding the difference between numbers. Perhaps this is because children are introduced to the minus sign as 'take away' and then have trouble relating it to 'how many more'? I have not found any infant age children who spontaneously represent such situations with a minus sign. I once asked two six year olds to show, in their own way, the game they were playing about finding the difference between two lots of counters, determined by a dice. Tania's record is rich in mathematically superfluous detail, clearly showing her interpretation of my request as referring to the whole context. Melanie, however, homed in on the counters, indicating the difference by colouring in (as her Fletcher maths book did). When asked if she could show the difference in a quicker way, she put a line between the 7 and 8, which might be seen either as a separator, or as an invented symbol for difference, like a minus sign on its side. She read what she had done as 'the difference between 7 and 8 is 1 '.

A similar symbol is used by Karen from Razia's class and read as, 'You need four to get from 2 up to 6'.

Karen also circles the difference number: this common device clearly seems to serve a punctuating function, of emphasising the result of the calculation. Both these methods seem to admirably fulfil their purpose of providing an economical record, to be shared by people who already know the context well. Perhaps this shows one of the dangers of encouraging children to use standard symbols before they are ready. It may be that we too easily assume that children understand the concepts behind the symbols, whereas to children the signs are just a way of keeping numbers apart.

Other children invent forms which reflect the apparatus used in the activity. One example of this is Koysor, who was finding the difference between pairs of numbers on a number line. She used a 'skipping rope' type representation, which seems to reflect an idea of the distance between the numbers, especially as she then chose to indicate the pair with the greatest difference by the longest line. This method is highly effective for representing the idea of 'difference', and certainly seems more helpful for young children than a minus sign.

Another example was Peter, aged 6, in Razia's class. He was playing a game of 'higher and lower' with a dice numbered to 20 and a butter bean coloured blue on one side. With 20 as his starting number for the activity, he threw the dice and bean together: if he threw blue and 16 he guessed what 16 higher than 20 was. If the bean came up white, he guessed 16 lower than 20. He then checked his results on the calculator. To represent this he used an arrow either going up or down, (interestingly, rejecting the calculator signs in favour of his own symbols). These seems to me a much more effective way of representing addition or subtraction, than the standard plus and minus symbols, which bear no relationship, visual or verbal, to the ideas that they represent, whereas the arrows reflect something of the essence of the operations. They may

also reflect the language of the activity, and Peter's previous experience with a wooden number ladder.

Children's difficulties with 'minus' in representing 'the difference' were underlined for me when I asked some children to select the appropriate keys on the calculator to check their results from the same practical game as Tania and Melanie played previously. Although they had been given more clues than children in the other activities, as far as having their options limited to the calculator keyboard, most children still had trouble, and started off adding the numbers. It was only by knowing the result that they were able to work out that it was the 'lowering key' they wanted, as one child put it. Those children who knew how to put two numbers into a calculator, and get a lower one on the display, could use the standard symbols to represent a practical problem. This seems to me one of the times when standard symbols are relevant and useful to young children: you need them to communicate with a calculator, if not with other people.

Finally, I would like to relate an example of a very young reception age child who demonstrated a readiness to use standard symbols in representing a practical problem. Some children were working with maths consultant Shirley Clarke on the 'school cook's problem'. This involved finding out what you could put on the children's plates if they were only allowed five things, and there were only eggs and chips. They had drawn pictures to represent the possibilities, added numbers to these, and then were asked if they wanted to write about what they had been doing. One child's writing, reproduced here, seems to show an awareness that numerals and plus signs are appropriate in this context. This seems to indicate that some young children already know a lot about mathematical communication, the forms it takes, and the kinds of things it is used for, in much the same way as they know a lot about what writing looks like and what it is used for, before they understand it fully. And some children, given half a chance, demonstrate a readiness to try out their knowledge of

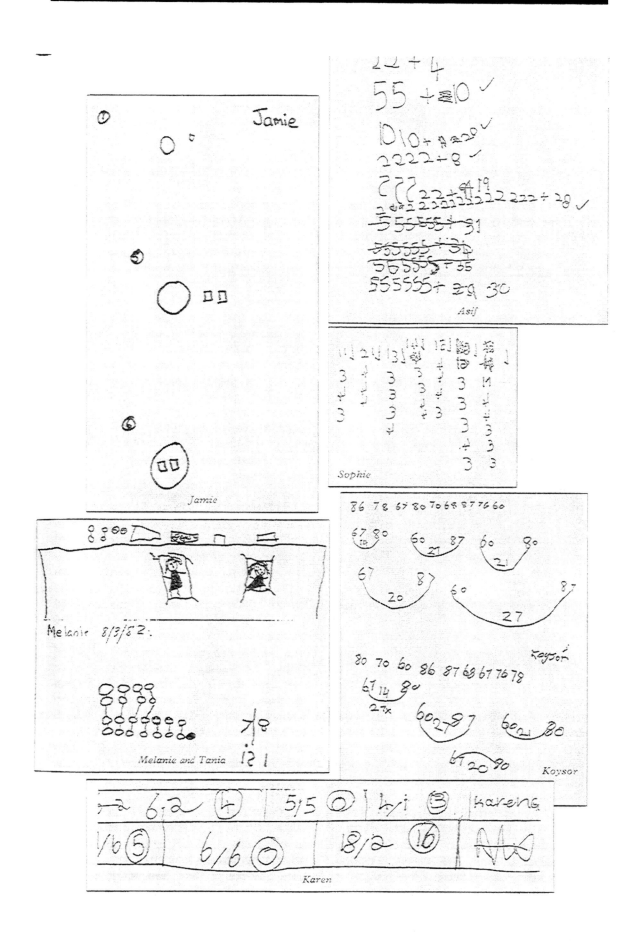

38

mathematical conventions. Is this because they have not yet learned a fear of failure, or been shown the 'correct' way to do things?

As regards this approach, I believe we can learn from current practice in teaching writing to young children, as proposed by the National Writing Project (1989). This emphasises:

- writing for real purposes rather than just assessment,

- teachers responding to the content rather than the form in the first instance, and

- setting up a classroom ethos where children respond to each other's work, and discuss and compare different forms.

As with the English NC Attainment Targets we could put more emphasis in maths activities on selecting a style which is appropriate to the audience and purpose. It also means creating an atmosphere where, although standard forms are known from an early age, doing your own thing is doing it 'right'.

So how does this approach fit in with mathematics teaching in the era of the NC? There are two main implications. Children using their own ways of recording mathematics are using notation systems that they understand and that are in their control. These systems give us valuable insights into the children's thinking and their understanding. On the other hand, children who are shown how to record may reveal only their compliance, rather than their understanding of operations and symbols. Secondly, we can use these insights to help children, and to move them on from non-standard forms whilst still maintaining understanding of what they are doing.

The NCC's Mathematics Non-Statutory Guidance emphasises the importance of children's own ways of working and recording:

"In developing skills in paper and pencil methods for calculations, pupils need to have opportunities to:

- record the results of operating with numbers in a variety of contexts and in a variety of ways, e.g. recording work done with structural apparatus;

- develop informal, personal methods of recording calculations with pencil and paper;

- compare and discuss different pencil and paper approaches to calculations."
(NCC, 1989, E.3-4)

If children are encouraged to use their own methods, to choose from a range of forms and discuss these choices, they will be in a better position to select the right form for the context and audience, or, as the NC puts it, 'be able to record findings and present them in oral, written, or visual form *as appropriate*' AT1 Level 4. Eventually this should make them better able, at Level 10, 'to use symbolisation with confidence'. Or was this what Asif and Peter, aged six, were doing?

References

1. Martin Hughes (1986) *Children and Number,* Oxford: Blackwell
2. Dufour-Janvier, et al (1987) *Pedagogical considerations concerning the problem of representation in* Janvier, C (ed) *Problems of representation in the teaching and learning of mathematics,* New Jersey: LEA
3. National Writing Project, (1989) *Becoming a Writer* 'Thomas Nelson & Son Ltd SCDC Publications
4. Open University (1982) EM235 *Developing Mathematical Thinking,* Milton Keynes: The Open University Press
5. NCC (1989) Mathematics Non-Statutory Guidance, York: NCC

Sue Gifford works at Roehampton Institute, London

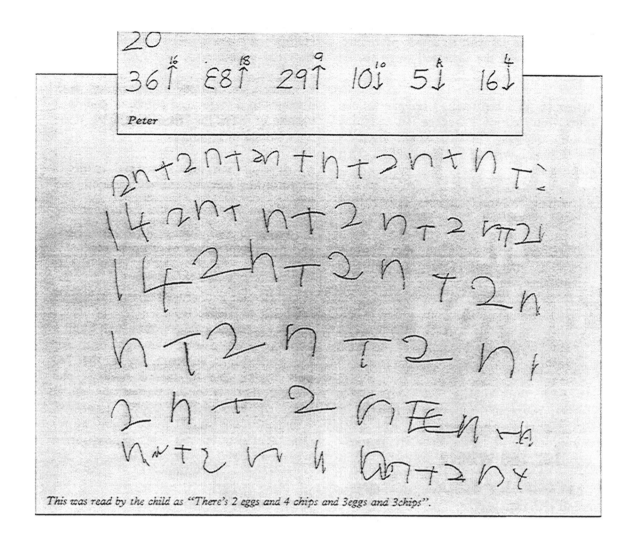

Peter

This was read by the child as "There's 2 eggs and 4 chips and 3 eggs and 3 chips".

The Primary Initiatives in Mathematics Education Project (PrIME) and its subsidiary project CAN were the most substantial primary mathematics development projects this country has known. **Janet Duffin** was an Evaluator of the CAN Project.

MATHEMATICS FOR THE NINETIES:
A calculator-aware number curriculum

I was fascinated to read, in MT133, about Viggo Hartz's closing lecture at last year's (1990) ATM Conference. The paragraph which stands out most in my mind is the one in which he said:

"... I am about to lead a project over the next three years aimed at giving up entirely the teaching of written algorithms for the four rules. We feel sure that giving children a pocket calculator as soon as they start school, and concentrating more on mental calculation, will give them greater competence."

In the same paragraph he also said: "In Denmark we do not carry out experiments in school, we do development work."

These two excerpts from his talk go right to the heart of work I have been doing in this country during the past four and a half years. Firstly because his description of what he is going to do in the next three years sums up so clearly and simply the spirit of the project I have been evaluating since January 1987. Secondly because his comment about Denmark suddenly illuminated for me a possible reason why it has not always been easy for teachers in this country to accept the terms of the project.

The background

The CAN (Calculator-Aware Number) project was set up in September 1986 with aims similar to those described by Viggo Hartz for Danish children. The project guidelines asked participating teachers not to teach the standard algorithms. Instead they were asked to develop mental facility alongside calculator use. At that stage no predictions were made about the outcome in terms of pupils' number competence, thoughts were rather on seeking a curriculum more appropriate to a calculator age than the current one.

The rationale behind the guidelines for the project came from a survey of practice in primary classrooms [1] together with evidence from surveys of number practice in adult life [2],[3]. The latter two found that heavy concentration on the standard algorithms in schools was not matched by adult practice.

In the first place the project was seen only as curriculum development and initiators and participants alike were unprepared for the dramatic changes which occurred amongst children and their teachers - except for those teachers who had, before the project came into being, already changed their teaching style in mathematics to fit more closely developments in practice in other areas of the primary curriculum.

Partly, perhaps because they could no longer put the emphasis on the teaching and practice of the standard algorithms which had been common before the start of the project (80% of the total time spent on number in primary school in England and Wales, the survey found), teachers were forced into listening to and observing their children in a way they had not done before in mathematics. A new teaching style began to emerge, one in which the teacher became less prescriptive, more an enabler and a facilitator, whose responsibility it then became to provide an environment in which the children would be free to develop their own strategies and thinking.

Some early subtraction methods

From a mixed group of 7 yr olds:

$135 - 72 = 63$

First I take 70 away from 100.
That leaves me with 30
Then I add the other 30 back.
That makes 60.
Then I take 2 from 5 that left 3
so the answer is 63.

TWO LESS ABLE CHILDREN AT 9 YRS

$72 - 58 = 14$
$70 - 50 = 20$
$2 - 8 = -6$
$20 - 6 = 14$

$96 - 34 = 62$
$96 - 10 = 86$
$86 - 10 = 76$
$76 - 10 = 66$
$66 - 4 = 62$

$90 - 36 = 56$

First I did 90 take away 30 and that come to 60 and then I did 0-6 and that came to -6 and then I added 60 and that come to 54.

$(364 - 47)$

$60 - 40 = 20$, add $4 = 24$, take $7 = 17$, add $300 = 317$.

First I did 61-20 and that came to 41 then I did 1-8 and it came to 33. $(61 - 28)$

Addition and Subtraction of larger numbers

TWO CHILDREN EXPLAINING THEIR SUBTRACTIONS

1. $31 - 17$

7 AND 8 IS 15, 15 AND 15 IS 30,
30 AND 1 IS 31, SO THE ANSWER
IS $8 + 15 + 1 = 24$

Q: WHY DO YOU START WITH 7 AND 8?

A: BECAUSE IT MAKES 15 AND 15 IS HALF OF 30

2. $32 - 19$

FIRST I THOUGHT I'D USE TILLICH BLOCKS AND THEN I THOUGHT I SHOULD DO IT IN MY HEAD. I PRETENDED THE 32 WAS 30 AND THE 19 WAS 20. 20 FROM 30 IS 10 SO THE ANSWER IS 3 MORE.

$765 + 143 + 289 = 1197$
$700 + 100 + 200 = 1000$
$60 + 40 + 80 = 180$
$5 + 3 + 9 = 17$

$4356 + 4165$
$4356 + 4100 = 8456$
$8456 + 65 = 8516$

$8.333 - 165 = 168$
$300 - 100 = 200$
$30 - 60 = -30$
$3 - 5 = -2$
$200 - 30 = 170$
$170 - 2 = 168$

$5534 - 3164$
$5534 - 3100 = 2434$
$2434 - 64 = 2370$

Children began to demonstrate the power of their thinking, partly because of this new approach on the part of their teachers, partly because of the kind of activities they were experiencing - more open-ended and investigatory than before. And out of these changes there also emerged the looked-for changes in the curriculum. It seems likely that these occurred mainly because of the freedom the calculator gave for exploration of numbers. This, alongside the new activities and new teacher attitudes, enabled such concepts as decimals and negative numbers to be encountered earlier than had hitherto been usual. The new way of working also began to make teachers question the standard ways of approaching some topics and concepts. Children's experience of place value, for example, was radically altered because of calculator use, as was their introduction to the idea of a negative number.

Perhaps because the new way of working was one which was already established in other areas of the curriculum for many primary teachers, difficulties encountered during the first three years of the project appeared largely, though not entirely, amongst those teachers for whom the change was revolutionary rather than developmental. But when the first children in the project got to within two years of secondary transfer, some teachers began to have doubts about the ban on the standard algorithms. They felt these would be expected by the secondary schools and that, without them, their children might be disadvantaged.

Autonomy and authority

It was at this stage that other questions, too, began to arise: questions about presentation, about refinement of children's methods to make them acceptable for later stages. Even in schools where hitherto the ban had presented no problems or queries, participants began to wonder whether these children should meet the standard algorithms before transferring to the secondary school and, if so, how this could be done within the project's original guidelines and within the teaching style which had evolved.

Almost since its beginning, an important element in the project has been the recognition that it is about autonomy: for the teacher, for the children, for the advisory teacher and for the evaluator. Everyone has been learning about their role in the project from their experience within it. So some teachers have been thinking of ways to handle the problem of what to do about children's diverse methods in an environment in which, they fear, standard methods may be expected. Others have a different view.

Sharing of methods amongst children has become common in CAN classrooms. Now some began to ask why, if it is appropriate for children to 'share' ideas and methods, it is not also appropriate for teachers to contribute their standard method. Nick James, after visits to several CAN schools, recognised the dilemma some teachers find themselves in. He had this to say:

"The teacher has to learn to give children autonomy. Instead of the teacher being the authority in the classroom, a climate must be created in which everyone's opinions have value and if teachers contribute their method before child autonomy is established, that method will be seen as authoritative and therefore to be accepted by all."

He went on to say that holding back on the part of the teacher can be very hard to learn.

Experimentation or development?

This is still an unresolved dilemma for some teachers and it is on this point that I find myself returning to Viggo Hartz's statement about not experimenting in Danish schools. Is it possible, I ask myself, that the dilemma stems from a feeling amongst some teachers that we are conducting experiments on the children and that is not acceptable? If we could be sure in England as they appear to be in Denmark that what is being done is developmental work rather than experimentation, it might be easier to overcome

Multiplying larger numbers

I got my numbers by turning 3, 1 digit cards over and shaking for my x – by – number, a 2 to 7 dice.

$$918 \times 3 = 2754$$
$$910 \times 3 = 2730$$
$$8 \times 3 = 24$$
$$2730 + 24 = 2754$$

I sometimes split my Hundreds, tens and units up, it really depends how I feel about the numbers.

– – – – –

This followed multiplication of 2 digit numbers on the calculator. The first attempt to work out 'how the calculator did it' ended with the answer 3240

$$54 \times 62 = 3348$$

Hour 4x

First I did 50 × 60 which came to 3000. Then I did 60 × 4 = 240 tr and then I added it on to 3000 which came to 3240. Then I did 50 × 2 which came to 100 and I added it on to 3240 which came to 3340 then I did 4 × 2 which came to ~~eight~~ and thats how it came to 3348.

the misgivings of genuinely doubting teachers.

Another aspect of this problem has recently arisen from the outcome of a questionnaire distributed to all participants with the idea that participant evaluation should be part of the autonomy which permeates the whole project.

The questionnaire, after a few questions related to factual information required to help with any analysis of the results, was composed mainly from comment and opinions expressed over the years by participants and others about the project. It was designed to ascertain attitudes of participants to such things as the algorithms; the children's and their own attitudes to the project; to concerns felt about such things as secondary transfer; parental attitudes; dissemination; children's knowledge of numbers facts; their strategies and their recording procedures, to name a few of the items contained in it.

A small case study was undertaken of nine late returns with the idea that a 'pilot' survey might bring out issues more difficult to discern in the larger study. I was quite startled by one thing which emerged from this sample. Amongst the nine respondents there were four who believed that the standard algorithms were still essential to the primary curriculum. These same four respondents also believed that, while the project had been beneficial to the able and the average children, it was not for the less able.

This was interesting, for one of the things which had emerged from talk with teachers, particularly those who were not sure of the wisdom of refraining from teaching algorithms, was that they felt that the standard algorithms were necessary for those children who did not find it easy to develop their own methods. Such children might be able to calculate reasonably competently in their heads and use a calculator when that proved difficult, but they could not devise a competent and economical way of recording a calculation. For example, some less able children could not find a method for subtraction

which would always work; some appear to be unable to move on from equal additions to finding a suitable method for multiplication.

There is no doubt that one of the concerns of teachers in every region has been about the need for all children to be able to refine their methods to produce a written procedure which would be acceptable at the secondary stage. The belief of some teachers appears to be that, where children fail to devise a satisfactory method for themselves they must be taught the standard methods.

For me this belief raises a very big question about the success of these standard methods in the community at large, judging by several recent reports used to castigate teachers and teaching methods. I find myself wondering about the usefulness of giving the standard procedures to those who have failed to devise their own because there is so much evidence that the less able - and some of the more able too - have never been able to remember them either in school or after they have left. It is an issue which must be debated both inside and outside the project.

But it is not on this aspect that I want to concentrate in this article. What I should like to do instead is to look at two examples of children's methods, both of which have something to tell us about the developmental nature of children's learning when it is given the opportunity to demonstrate itself through a teaching style which is prepared to await that development.

Development of a subtraction method

On a visit to a CAN school during the first year of the project I was shown a piece of work done by a 6/7 year old.

$$\begin{array}{r} 427 \\ -259 \\ \hline 232 \end{array}$$

(and, written at the side:
But the real answer is 168.)

Some division methods

$78 \div 3 = 26$

$20 + 20 + 20 = 60$ ✓

$8 \div 3 = 2 \text{ rem } 2$

$10 \div 3 = 3 \text{ rem } 1$

$2 + 1 = 3$

$3 \div 3 = 1$ ✓

$179 \div 2 = 89 \text{ r} 1$
$100 \div 2 = 50$
$70 \div 2 = 35$
$9 \div 2 = 4 \text{ r} 1$

$45 \div 3 = 15$

$10 \times 3 = 30$

$3 \times 5 = 15$ ✓

$15 \times 3 = 45$

$2140 \div 160$
$160 \times 10 = 1600$
$160 \times 11 = 1760$
$160 \times 13 = 2080$
$160 \times 14 = 2240$

$36 \div 5 = 7 \text{ r} 1 \ (0.2)$

$56 \div 3 = 18 \text{ r} 2 \ (0.66 \rightarrow)$

$65 \div 3 = 21 \text{ r} 2 \ (0.66 \rightarrow)$

$63 \div 5 = 12 \text{ r} 3 \ (0.6)$

$35 \div 6 = 5 \text{ r} 5 \ (0.83 \rightarrow)$

$53 \div 6 = 8 \text{ r} 5 \ (0.83 \rightarrow)$

$219 \div 7 = 31.3$
$8.60 \times 7 = 200.2$
$70 \times 7 = 19.4$
$200.2 + 19.4 = 219.6$

This sum began to drive me up the wall, but I've now done the answer on the calculator and it did not come to 31.3 instead it came to 31.285714...I couldn't for the life of me work that out in my head, or even on the calculator I wouldn't think of putting that in.

$279 \div 8 = 34.875$
$200 \div 8 = 25$
$70 \div 8 = 8.75$
$9 \div 8 = 1.125$

I asked the child about this. Unfortunately it had been done a few weeks previously and he had forgotten why he wrote that.

I gave him another to do. This time he wrote down

$$\begin{array}{r} 524 \\ -278 \\ \hline -354 \end{array}$$

I pointed out that this was a different kind of answer from the one he had given before. His reply was 'Oh, I didn't know about negative numbers then' but he was still not able to explain much more about his answer.

I tried him on two digit questions: 74 - 38. He told me:

seventy take away thirty is 40
four take away eight is -4
so the answer is 44

Before he gave me his final answer I thought he was on to a valid way to subtract and I was disappointed with his reply. I took it no further that day. When I returned the following term he was satisfactorily applying a correct procedure with both two and three digit subtractions. His way of recording was as above except that his answer would now be 36.

I considered the stages through which his development seemed to have gone.

First: a strategy of subtracting the smaller digit from the larger for each column, a method which did not give him the answer which his own internal logic told him was the right answer. I wondered where the conflicting logic of always taking the smaller from the larger came from. On another occasion with another child I thought I had seen the reason why: at the concrete stage of encountering subtraction, children always 'take away a smaller number' of objects from those they have in front of them. And even if originally they meet other manifestations of subtraction this seems to be the one which persists when the concrete is overtaken by recording the process. It is comparatively easy to think of ways in which calculator use could undermine this early perception.

Replaced by: a strategy which had a different consistency: if you start by taking the top digit from the bottom digit then you must do that for all digits which would account for the "-" in front of the answer in the second presentation.

Leading to an intermediate stage, when operating with the negative numbers produced is not yet fully established, leading on to a competent algorithm which can handle the negative numbers sometimes generated. It is perhaps interesting to note here that, while most CAN children who use this method write it out as above, in some work done under the Wiskobas scheme, children in Netherlands write this method as follows:

$$\begin{array}{r} 437 \\ -289 \\ \hline \overset{-\,-}{252} \\ \hline 148 \end{array}$$

Many CAN children seem to calculate from the left instead of from the right as in the standard methods. I was puzzled about why this should be until I was once talking with another child who had told me about his way for adding 27 and 46: twenty and forty are sixty, seven and six are thirteen so he answer is seventy three. Asked what he had used to help him to do this, he got out sets of ten connected cubes and individual cubes and after laying them out in front of me, he picked up the tens cubes first. On being shown that, it seemed obvious that one would pick up the bigger pieces of equipment first. In the abstract it is not so obvious because we are so tied to the standard ways of calculating.

So it appears, that by being given the freedom to develop and mature without interference children can come to a compact and elegant method for a process which standard procedures previously denied to all those except the ones who were always prone to devising their own methods. The big difference is that previously, as I know from work with undergraduates, there was a tendency for these self-devised methods to be kept hidden for fear of censure. Now they can be made public they are more likely to spread amongst those who may not be able to devise a competent method for themselves.

Two ways towards place value understanding

My other example demonstrates that ways towards understanding may not be the same for all children. I was with a group of children who were doubling. One girl told me that she had got as far as 512. She said she had done up to 64 in her head and remembered 128 because she had done it last week but that the other two she had done on her calculator. I asked her if she thought she could do the next one in her head. She was doubtful but a boy sitting near said: "It'll be ten hundred and twenty four and the next one will be two thousand and 48." I asked him to key his numbers into his calculator. He showed me 200048. Meantime the girl had got there by doing it on her calculator and told me correctly what the number was. They compared their displays and were nonplussed.

I was not able to follow up this episode but it interested me greatly that these two children both had some understanding of place value and both had some deficiency in their ability to handle the processes they were working with. The boy was more competent mentally and could translate from hundreds to thousands accurately but he did not know how to record his answer correctly; the girl failed to do the mental calculation but could read correctly the answers her calculator gave her. In a classroom which recognises the right of children to develop towards competence through their own efforts and in their own way, such examples are likely to occur often and suggest that a preconceived view of a 'correct' way towards mastery of a procedure may not be conducive to maximum achievement for all children.

So besides my initial reasons for starting by quoting from Viggo Hartz's article I am also delighted to find that there are other countries now looking at similar things to ourselves. Denmark, the Netherlands and Australia are three countries where I know these developments are taking place.

It will be interesting to see if similar problems to those we have been encountering arise in these other projects. We may then be in a better position to determine whether problems are unique to this country or occur similarly for other countries. Either way we are likely to be better equipped to see how to overcome those common problems which do arise.

Nevertheless, in spite of our difficulties I still believe this is a development for the future and I hope that those teachers willing and able to take on board the ideas, philosophy and practice of the CAN project will be able to go on from strength to strength showing us that English children are not so innumerate as some in the community tend to believe them to be.

Notes:

1. The Wiskobas scheme was a developmental project in the Netherlands, and the method used by Dutch children can be found in the proceedings of the 1988 Annual Conference of the Psychology of Mathematics Education group.

2. Nick James worked in mathematics education at the Open University for a number of years.

3. Projects similar to CAN have been started in both Tasmania and Victoria, Australia. Two linked projects were launched in the Netherlands about a year ago, one university based, the other in school.

References

1. Hilary Shuard, *Mathematics today and tomorrow,* Longmans 1986
2. Bridget Sewell, *Uses of mathematics by adults in daily life,* ACAE, 1982
3. Tony Fitzgerald, *New technology and mathematics in employment,* 1985
4. Viggo Hartz, *Mathematics and democracy: a real problem,* MT133

Janet Duffin is CAN Evaluator, at the CAN Continuation Project, Homerton College, Cambridge

The teaching of number is a perennial concern of teachers, parents and the Government. **Alan Wigley** goes back to basics.

TEACHING NUMBER: A RADICAL RE-APPRAISAL

After many years of studying the subject, some radical thoughts about the teaching and learning of number begin to crystallise in the mind. Although none is original in itself, they do fit together in a way which suggests that primary schools could be helped to transform the teaching of number for the better. This article concentrates mostly on the pure aspects of number (and early computation in particular), leaving measures and applications to some other occasion.

To begin, we must agree on a premise which, hopefully, is acceptable in an age when calculators are available for most practical purposes. The premise is that the ability to compute mentally reflects a grasp of the number system which is both fundamental to mathematical thinking and also necessary for sensible use of a calculator.

Mental methods are characteristically variable, but consider for a moment the way in which many people will do the sum 23 + 45 in their heads:

"Twenty-three and forty-five ... twenty and forty makes sixty ... three and five makes eight ... sixty and eight makes sixty-eight." Three important features of this simple procedure are:

- Understanding of the language of numbers is used to decompose, combine and recompose them;
- Knowledge of number bonds is used, without resort to counting;
- The order for calculating corresponds to that for reading, namely from left to right.

Weak aspects of the prevailing model for teaching number reside in the failure to develop satisfactorily the three features

just described: this is so where the language of numbers is taught in small steps using questionable physical models, often leaving pupils devoid of adequate understanding; where number bonds are taught unimaginatively and inefficiently, with regressive counting methods being allowed, even encouraged, by the materials offered; and where, as is often the case, the order for reading numbers is ignored altogether when calculating!

These are not the only weaknesses in the prevailing model, however. Much early work, which sometimes masquerades under the title 'pre-number' is based on questionable premises. These will be examined briefly before moving to a consideration of the issues listed above.

Pre-number: a false start

Early work of dubious value to the development of number understanding includes activities such as sorting objects into sets or ordering them according to selected criteria, and matching objects one-to-one. Such activities derive from a belief that the logical structure of set theory, used in the late 19th and early 20th centuries to re-examine the foundations of mathematics, would also apply to number learning by young children. The adoption of this theoretical perspective had disguised a more natural beginning to number, such as a child's parent might use with them, namely counting. Two ideas have been over-formalised, the notion of a set and the associated idea of one-to-one correspondence.

A notoriously influential example was derived from some of Piaget's experiments in which young children's answers to questions were interpreted as indicating an inability to 'conserve' number. Yet, on what evidence do we come to believe that a child thinks that if some sweets are spread out then they have 'gained' some sweets, or that if they are lumped together, then they have 'lost' some?

How can we be certain that responses are not more to do with the child's interpretation of words such as 'more' and 'less' in a particular context, rather than any fundamental misconception? [1] At some stage, counting collections, checking and discussing whether you agree with other people becomes of real interest in the classroom. But there is no need to devise activities to teach conservation or for the teacher to wait until children are 'ready'!

Counting begins with learning number names in order, and then counting sets of objects by reciting the sequence of number names in coordination with successive pointing at objects. Note that:

- If number names are learned first, the learner can then give undivided attention to coordinating the number names with the 'pointing'. By delaying counting objects until later and treating the matter more informally, the often excessive amount of time given to counting objects can be reduced.

- Synchronising two sequential actions, one of which requires careful attention to ensure that each object is pointed to once and once only, is different from and more complex in nature than simple one-to-one matching. It is learned effectively when there is the motivation to count things. Prior experience of matching activities is not required to achieve this purpose and does not help anyway.

Notation: beginning with the language of numbers

Learning should begin with the names of numbers to 10 in an ordered sequence. After that, I have two concerns about the way in which teachers often proceed:

1. *Step-by-step building up from small numbers to bigger numbers.* This fails to give pupils an overview of the system and insight into the regularity with which numbers are written. Also, because irregularities in the way in which we say numbers in English are concentrated mostly in the second decade, a step-by-step approach presents hurdles which slow the learning.

2. *Efforts to explain place value by grouping and exchanging objects in tens.* This is supposed to make an abstract idea concrete, which now seems to be a somewhat odd notion. After all, place value is not a property of any physical material - it is simply a notational device, a pattern of linguistic usage. How materials are meant to be manipulated has to be learned and there is no necessary connection between what is done, with base ten blocks for example, and how we write numbers. Ten-rods clearly look different from unit cubes, whereas 'place value' is a reference to the fact that the same mark (digit) is read differently according to its position in a number! In fact, the translation from one context to the other is not at all obvious and does not explain place value, which has to make sense in itself, not through some external reference. [2]

An alternative approach is offered by Caleb Gattegno [3], who argues that place value should be treated as a part of *language* learning and proposes working directly on the notation in a systematic and effective way. Because this approach is fundamentally different from current practice it is worth outlining the early stages in a little detail. He begins by building up a 'tens table' in the following manner.

Using a wall chart with a pointer, first teach children to say the numbers from 1 to 9, in order and randomly:

1   2   3   4   5   6   7   8   9

Practise this to fluency.

By adding the sound 'hundred' a lot more numbers can be spoken:

1   2   3   4   5   6   7   8   9

100 200 300 400 500 600 700 800 900

By successive pointing it is possible to say, for example, 'five hundred and seven'. Working together, practise to fluency.

Introducing the sound 'ty', add these in the middle row:

1   2   3   4   5   6   7   8   9
           40   60 70 80 90
100 200 300 400 500 600 700 800 900

Having learned these new sounds, build up to examples such as 'eight hundred and sixty-seven'.

Three more can be added with a slight alteration to the sound each time, eg we say 'twenty' rather than 'two-ty':

1   2   3   4   5   6   7   8   9
    20 30 40 50 60 70 80 90
100 200 300 400 500 600 700 800 900

Proceed as before, again to achieve fluency.
Finally, add the 'ten', for which one might temporarily adopt the sound 'one-ty':

1   2   3   4   5   6   7   8   9
10 20 30 40 50 60 70 80 90
100 200 300 400 500 600 700 800 900

Notice how this approach overcomes the objections raised. Working with the numbers up to a 1000 in this tabular layout exposes the underlying structure which our compact notation hides (eg 537 = 500 + 30 + 7) and sets the irregularities in the *spoken* language in a more general context where regularity predominates. Also, it is purely a language exercise - there is no attempt to extract place value as a property of something, eg by using rods and blocks.

One advantage of the table is that the sounds of numbers are learned before the compact notation is introduced. Exercises for reading and writing numbers might be devised using materials such as 'arrow cards', a set of 27 cards which correspond to the numbers in the table.

To illustrate, the following cards would be placed on top of each other (ie arrow heads together) to show 537:

The cards expose in a very visual way what lies hidden when we write numbers conventionally, here 537 meaning 500 + 30 + 7. It is this notational convention which learners need to internalise, reading the '3' as 'thirty' rather than '3 in the tens column'.

The final step in acquiring the language of numbers is to learn how to order them. The traditional hundred square is useful as an aid to counting up and down the sequence starting at various points, it being largely unnecessary to practice this for numbers above 100.

Number bonds: moving away from counting

It has been said that the greater part of mathematics has been motivated by the search for clever ways of counting. Certainly it is true that efficient arithmetical computation exploits two capabilities:
1. use of the language structure for naming numbers (sometimes called place value) and
2. quick recall/rapid reconstruction of number bonds.

Place value has been discussed; what about learning number bonds? At the outset, it should be stressed that rapid reconstruction of facts is just as important as direct 'recall' - efficient use of memory implies a mix of methods which necessarily varies from one individual to another. Again, there are two major weaknesses:

- Lack of confidence on the part of teachers and a paucity of ideas for working with the class together, in ways which would contribute to understanding and fluency in processes.
- The use of inappropriate concrete materials in individual and small group work.

The need for systematic and rigorous class work on the language of numbers has already been stressed, and the same can be said for acquisition of number bonds. This means going beyond just chanting tables or testing with random questions. A structured approach will help children to 'fix' certain facts such as 5 + 5 = 10 (fingers on two hands) and to establish others by employing quick mental transformations of known facts (eg 6 x 5 from 5 x 5, + 5). Gattegno suggests the use of folded fingers to learn the addition and subtraction bonds to 10. Thus, with hands spread out and four fingers folded down, we have available to us the facts 4+6=10, 10-4=6 and 10-6=4. There is no counting involved, rather the imprinting of an image which holds the fact ("fingers in the mind", one child said).

Multiplication facts need to be tackled in such a way as to emphasise the underlying structure. For example, following exercises to teach doubling and halving (skills which many people learn readily) this table with blanks could be used:

	1	2	3	4	5	6	7	8	9	10
×2	*	*	*	*	*	*	*	*	*	*
×4	*	*	*	*	*	*	*	*	*	*
×8	*	*	*	*	*	*	*	*	*	*

Pointing in systematic ways to sequences of blank cells is used to trigger responses with the appropriate product, whilst at the same time developing awareness of the structure, and ability to use interrelationships between the entries in the table.

Oral work needs to be complemented by individual or small group work, when pupils can explore simple number relationships and patterns. However, many hours are wasted in classrooms by using materials which are inappropriate because they do not help the learner to move beyond inefficient counting methods. For example, one sees children working on problems such as 5+8, setting out a block of 5 cubes, another of 8 cubes and then combining them and counting them individually to get a total.

What they are learning here is simply bad habits! Number lines are fashionable, but as a computational aid their use might only reinforce the strategies of 'counting on' and 'counting back', which are still inefficient. It is true that we all sometimes regress to these more primitive strategies, whether through lack of confidence, because our attention is divided, or simply because they are entirely appropriate to the particular context (eg moving your counter on in a board game). There is nothing wrong with this, but children must be taught to develop more advanced methods - having begun arithmetic by learning to count, it then becomes necessary to discourage counting! Tall and Gray in their article in MT142 make a clear distinction between a number as the total derived from a count and a number as an object which can be combined within other numbers in flexible ways. The reader is referred to their article for a more detailed discussion of the point. [4]

What then is the solution to this problem with materials for representing number? Briefly, digital formats are to be preferred: tabular arrays and sequences, number cards of various kinds, calculators, dice, etc. As has been shown by the CAN project and other experience, calculators have a vital part to play. Problems with larger numbers, where trial and improvement methods are needed, can be used to promote intelligent exploration and use of the number system. (For example, 'find ways of getting from 27 to 54 using the addition key', 'find three numbers which add up to 100', etc.). If one is looking for a more concrete or visual analogue, then Cuisenaire rods are one material which does not reinforce primitive methods: since each number is represented by an unsegmented rod, learners are encouraged to see numbers as undivided entities.

Computation: connecting with mental processes

The third step is to consider how understanding of number notation and knowledge of number bonds are used in computation with bigger numbers. Prior to the availability of calculators and computers it was necessary for people to perform complex computations on paper - quickly, accurately, compactly and repeatedly. This is no longer the case. Today, what is required is a flexible range of mental methods in order to be able to estimate, make rough checks and understand how the number system works. This need not exclude the use of pencil and paper; after all, we often use paper as an aide memoire and jot down intermediate results which are difficult to hold in our heads. And even where a calculator would normally be used (e.g. 84 x 35) it seems important that pupils should be able to develop an approach to tackling a problem by breaking it down into a series of steps. It follows that there is value in developing a variety of pencil-and-paper methods seen as an extension of mental methods.

The major block to progress is the persistence of traditional written methods of working from right to left, when mental methods invariably work from left to right. This has led to strenuous efforts to explain the processes of 'borrowing' and 'carrying' of detached digits, often using

complex exchanges with materials such as base 10 blocks.

My criticism of this is twofold:
- it detaches the learner from a range of ingenious personal mental methods based on understanding of how numbers are composed;
- it also introduces extraneous explanations based on manipulating physical materials, which do not enhance understanding.

The need to connect with mental methods suggests initially getting pupils to record and share with each other their own methods for tackling problems [5]. Often they will compute as they read, starting on the left with the most significant digit. Furthermore, problems set in a context where the operation is not specified, are often tackled in a startling variety of ways.

For example, a question in the Key Stage 2 trial SATs (1993) asked how many 57-seater buses would be needed to carry 200 children and 15 adults on a trip. Below two eleven-year-olds show their working, neither using division:

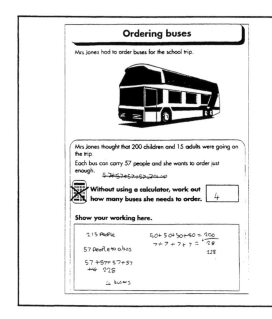

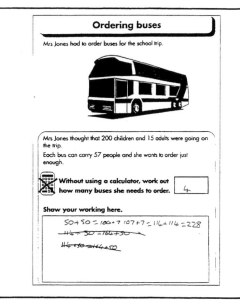

Ian Thompson's article 'Thirteen ways to solve a problem' in MT 144 (September 1993) [6] gives a fascinating description of different children's explanations of how they solved the problem: 'The garden wall has 4 rows of bricks. Each row has 144 bricks. How many bricks are there?' Ian notes that most pupils use addition or some form of doubling, rather than direct multiplication. Thus although 'what is 144 x 4?' may invoke a traditionally taught algorithm, the context of this problem elicited a rich variety of individual approaches based on principles understood by the pupils. This accords with research on the use of arithmetic in the workplace and provides yet another reason for encouraging efficient, personal and understood methods.

Pupils need *considerable* experience, over several years, of recording, sharing and refining their informal methods. At an appropriate time, it should be feasible to discuss some vertical formats, based on the principle of decomposing numbers as they are read. Particular methods should not be imposed - there is no point in replacing one set of poorly-understood methods by another!

Of the *'Ordering Buses'* examples shown, the first reads like this:

'300 and 200 is 500,
60 and 70 is 130,
5 and 8 is 13,
500 and 100 is 600,
30 and 10 is 40,
and 3 gives 643'

This mental 'patter' is important: it is in the link between the patter and what is written that understanding actually lies.

Subtraction is often done by some form of complementary addition (example 2 shows one way), but a novel approach is shown in example 3. It requires the use of negative numbers (30 - 70 = - 40 and 2 - 9 = - 7), but this is not strange to pupils who have used a calculator from an early age:

		632 − 279			632
365					−279
+ 278		279			
		280	1		400
500		300	20		−40
130		600	300		−7
13		632	32		
					360
643			353		−7
					353

Since the traditional formal methods no longer need to be taught, grouping and exchanging using concrete materials (counters, cubes, blocks, or whatever) become redundant activities. 'Borrowing' and 'carrying' detached digits, which for many have always remained part of a mysterious process, will have only historical interest! [7]

Towards a new model for teaching number

Effective teaching of number needs a structured and progressive approach, which also gives children scope to explore numbers and find their own ways of solving problems. To be rigorous and stimulating, schemes of work must be based on an adequate theoretical model. Traditional teaching of number was heavily based on repetition of teacher-given processes. I do not want that. The supposedly more insightful methods of the sixties and onwards were based on Piagetian notions of stages of development and attempts to explain processes using concrete materials. I do not want that. I should like to take from the former something which I think we have lost, namely the social practice of chanting. (I recall a remark by Dick Tahta, to the effect that chanting is a meaningful feature of many ritual observances where people gather together [8].) Also, the desire to develop efficient methods of computation.

I should like to take from the latter, the desire that children should understand, but with a different sense of meaning. Also, the encouragement for them to explore and gain enjoyment from pattern in number. The model I have in mind would initially induct children into the language patterns of the number system. Then, drawing on the understanding they derive from using the language, it would develop a flexible range of mental methods which learners explain to each other and refine together.

After 20 years of calculators in schools, the theories and practices of the past still have a firm, if not always clear, hold on the educational establishment. A different approach offers the possibility of simultaneously raising standards of achievement and saving precious time. If it is to be seriously tested some deeply embedded beliefs have to be challenged.

References

1. Many educational psychologists have looked critically at aspects of Piaget's theory. V. Walkerdine, in *The Mastery of Reason* (Routledge, 1988, ISBN 0 415 05233 5) addresses some of the contextual problems of language and the way in which children's thinking is affected by their social experience.
2. In each section of this article I question the appropriateness of many concrete materials currently used in the teaching of number, particularly attempts to embody the concept of place value. Recent writers contrast such attempts to give meaning to mathematical ideas with the meaning which derives from patterns of language use and the eventual requirement to achieve fluency in manipulating mathematical expressions independently of any external reference. (See for example the discussions of metaphor and metonym in Tahta [8] or in Walkerdine [1]).
3. Gattegno has been a key influence. Reading the early pages of *The Science of Education, part 2b: the awareness of mathematization* (Educational Solutions, 1988, ISBN 0 87825195 2) inspired this article.
4. E. Gray and D. Tall, MT 142: *Success and failure in mathematics - the flexible meaning of symbols as process and concept.*
5. H. Ginsberg, *Children's arithmetic* (Van Nostrand, 1977), gives many examples of the unfortunate gap which often exists between children's informal understanding of number and the written arithmetic they do in school.
6. I. Thompson, MT144: *Thirteen ways to solve a problem.*
7. A significant article on computational algorithms was that by S. Plunkett, *Decomposition and all that rot*, published originally in Mathematics in schools (8:3), reprinted in a joint ATM/MA publication entitled *'Calculators in the primary school'*
8. D. Tahta, 1991: *Understanding and desire*, an article in *Teaching and learning school mathematics*, Hodder and Stoughton, ISBN 0 340 56791 0, an OU course reader edited by D. Pimm and E. Love. Dick Tahta develops many of the themes taken up in my article. He also handled the manuscript for Gattegno's last book. [3]

Alan Wigley, Adviser for Mathematics, Wakefield LEA.

Eddie Gray and **Demetra Pitta** are certain that calculators are not bad for the mathematical health of eight-year-olds.

CHANGING EMILY'S IMAGES

Introduction

Symbolism has the power to dually and ambiguously represent processes to *do* and concepts to *know* [1]. To benefit from the flexibility provided by such ambiguity the young child's conception of arithmetic must progress through several phases of compression: lengthy counting procedures which are interpretations of processes to *do* must eventually become concepts to *know*.

This is a story of an eight-year-old who had considerable difficulty in simple arithmetic. Though she could use real things to help her sort out mathematical combinations, she had begun to feel that arithmetic should be done in her head. However, her efforts to do so did not lead to successful outcomes. Her mental approaches relied heavily upon the manipulation of imaginistic objects: analogues of the very things she was trying to move away from. It was hypothesised that if the 'procedural clutter' associated with her physical interpretation of mathematical symbols could be removed, she too could focus on the power of symbols. To do this we provided her with a graphic calculator, the 'supercalculator'. Our focus is the opportunity that the resource may give for stimulating the construction of mental imagery associated directly with arithmetical symbols as opposed to imagery that is an analogical transformation of them.

Pitta and Gray have described how children at extreme levels of achievement in elementary arithmetic focus on imagery which is of different qualities. Imagery identified by 'high achievers' tended to be symbolic, used to support the production of known facts or the numeric transformations which produce derived

facts. Imagery reported by 'low achievers' was usually based on analogical representations of physical objects. These images appear to be clear imitations of actions that could have taken place with real objects. The issue for this paper is whether an alternative 'procedure' may discourage a 'low achiever' from using manipulatives in the mind and instead stimulate the creation and construction of symbolic images that help to generate thought.

We first met Emily in February 1995. She had considerable difficulty with elementary arithmetic. Articulate and highly motivated, she was identified as one of the lowest achievers within her year group of 119 children. Test results placed her amongst the bottom four children. Our initial conversations with her were about the numbers 1 to 10. Her responses were dominated by descriptions of images that were analogues of physical objects. She relied extensively on active mental images to deal with elementary number combinations. If these involved combinations greater than ten Emily made considerable use of her fingers.

Emily saw the numbers one to six as mental arrays of dots in the mind very much like those arranged on a die. It is very possible that extensive experience with board games supplied the basis for these. Emily explained:
When I was young, when it was winter, we often played board games because we were not allowed outside. We were using dice. We were playing all of the time using dice.

Numbers between seven and ten were mental images of fingers arranged in a linear fashion. Emily manipulated her mental images of dots, her preferred image, relatively easily.

The solution to 4 - 3 was explained as:

As I see it there's two dots above each other and then there's ... the first one, the one below and the one next to it are being taken away and there is only one left up at the top.

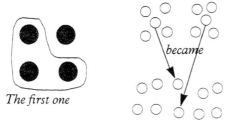

The first one

For 5+5 Emily described how she could take away the dot from the middle of the five and put it in the middle of the five and put it in line with the twos. She now had a line *"with five lots of two and I can see that is ten"*.

Emily recognised that there was much greater difficulty associated with her 'finger like' images. Using these meant doing two things at once, counting and concentrating on the sequence in which each finger was used:

I am trying to think out the answer as well as use all of my fingers - this is confusing ... with the dots it is easier [than with fingers] because you don't have to keep thinking, 'No it's that one I need to move, no, its that one, or that one ... [with the dots] it doesn't matter which you move.

It seemed as if the arrangement of the dots was allowing her to immediately see the amount in the set whereas the linear arrangement of fingers forced her to count.

Emily seemed to associate counting with fingers with the use of a sequence of particular fingers. When she used mental images of the dots she implied that she could use any dots.

For relatively more difficult combinations such as 'nine take away six' Emily used her fingers in an indirect way by 'feeling' them without looking at them, touching them or moving them. But Emily did not like using her fingers:

I find it easier not to do it with my fingers at times because sometimes I get into a big muddle with them because I find it much harder to add up because I am not concentrating on the sum. I am concentrating on getting my fingers right ... which takes a while. I can take longer to work out the sum than it does to work out the sum in my head.

Emily appeared to recognise that there was a qualitative difference between using perceptual items and mental representations of these items. It was not only that she believed the latter was easier, but to her it also showed the difference between 'doing' arithmetic and 'thinking' about arithmetic:

I try not to use my hands much... I don't bother looking because I am too busy thinking so... when I am not using my hands I am trying to work the sum out.

Overall, Emily's experience had led her to some conclusions about simple arithmetic. First, she felt it was easier to do the sum in her head and second, some images were better than others. It seemed to her that it was easier to see a number and remember it if it was recognised by some form of pattern like the array on a die. It was harder to think about if the representation was based upon a line of finger-like objects, each being focused upon at a separate point in the counting procedure. Third, arithmetic involved being seen to be 'doing', but this was unsettling because she was trying to 'think'. Unfortunately, however, she was not thinking with the tools her more able peers were using, the arithmetical symbols. Her tools were analogical images of real objects manipulated in accordance with her recollections of former experiences. Numerical symbols were concretised to form objects which supported the use of mental imagery that was episodic and active. Her focus was on an action which could be simplified by the nature of the representation that she gave to the objects. However, whether or not she used dots, fingers or finger-like objects the intrinsic quality of the object did not change. Her perception of quantity influenced her choice of objects and the way the objects were used, and so the focus turned to the nature of the action. But the action was always the same - counting. Though it was evident that her procedural competence was sound, it had not supported the encapsulation of numerical processes into concepts. She was not filtering out unnecessary information and making the cognitive shift that would lead to the realisation that symbols could become objects of thought. Unless some alternative pedagogy was tried, the longer term prognosis for Emily's achievement was that the qualitative difference between Emily's thinking and that of her more able peers would widen into a gulf. A graphic calculator was to be the tool for this pedagogy.

An alternative procedure: focusing on symbols

Contrary to the belief in many quarters that calculators have caused a decline in the ability of children to handle basic arithmetic, it has been recognised for some time that calculators can give children an insight into numerical patterns and relationships that are hard to discern if children are constrained by the use of lengthy counting procedures or the knowledge of isolated number combinations.

The graphic calculator - after Ken Ruthven [2] we called it a 'supercalculator' - seems to have an added advantage in this field. Combinations can be recorded and displayed in their entirety and equivalent outcomes from different procedures may also be seen at the same time. In addition, the child can control the form of display on the screen.

$4 + 5$	9
$4 + 4 + 1$	9
$3 + 2 + 4$	9

Graphic Calculator Display: Combinations to 9

For our attempt to minimise Emily's focus on counting the supercalculator offered two strengths; it provided an alternative procedure, pressing buttons, and it also had the potential to provide an alternative representation for numbers: it could display all symbols and operations at the same time. It was conjectured that this would offer an opportunity for Emily to stop counting and concentrate on numerical symbols as objects of thought. This, it was conjectured, would provide a stimulus which would support mental organisation.

A calculator provides an opportunity to create a number by pressing a button. It also permits a particular number to be created using a composite sequence of button pressing. Thus, when a child is asked to create 9, this can be done by pressing $4 + 5 =$, by pressing $6 + 3 =$ or it can be formed from $2 + 3 + 4$ or $13 - 4$, etc. By eliminating a counting procedure the alternative procedure had the potential to create a 'wholeness' about number. This may be seen at two levels; a specific one in which the focus could be on number triples, such as 4, 5, 9, and a more generic one during which it is possible to identify the relationships between numbers and simple operations, for example 9 is $4 + 5$, or $12 - 3$, or $10 - 4 + 3$, etc. It is unfortunately the case that many 'low achievers' find it hard to switch from harder to easier methods if the first is habitual and unfamiliar. The button pressing procedure had the potential to overcome this difficulty.

Emily was introduced to the supercalculator in April 1995. The programme built around its use was not seen as simply another way of doing things. The calculator was not a means for completing the result of arithmetical combinations, but a way of seeking different combinations that made a particular number. Emily's mental or physical procedures provide her with one route to a number. The calculator provides an infinite number of routes. Thus, she started with the number and considered alternative ways to obtain it. Four phases were established to support Emily's development:

- Emily is given an opportunity to think about numbers without using the calculator.
- The calculator is used to support thinking, not simply to check answers. Emily could control the form of the numbers and seeing one

combination maintained in display she could try the same numbers with a different button-pressing procedure. Memory usually associated with holding quantities and carrying out counting procedures could be directed towards thinking about number combinations.

- At the end of each activity she could consider interesting things that had been discovered during the activity.
- She was given an opportunity to talk about individual numerals and associated combinations.

To accompany her work a specially personalised booklet was designed with each page following a pattern similar to that shown. The programme called for Emily to try to complete a page of her booklet each week.

Each week she discussed her work with the programme designers. During this time she was asked to talk about her numbers without access to the calculator or to her written responses.

Programme development

Initially Emily had to overcome some reluctance to use the calculator. This stemmed largely from her perception of what others may think. However, by the end of the first week she had established that there were many ways in which she could make nine, the first number in the booklet. There were, of course, standard addition combinations such as 4 + 5, 3 + 6, etc, but she also provided others, 4 + 4 + 1, 3 + 4 + 2, and using the starting points of 5 and 10 she could provide solutions such as, 5 + 1 + 1 + 2, 5 + 5 - 1, 5 + 6 - 2, 10 - 1. Emily admitted that she wouldn't have thought of these sorts of combinations earlier, but her outstanding discovery for the week was that she had found out that she could add larger numbers and then take away

"I didn't know that you could add larger number and then take away. I didn't know you could go up and down."

```
Working with nine . . . .
                                    9
Making nine                1._____
2._____               3._____
4._____               5._____
Working with the calculator
Ways to make nine
1._____               2._____
3._____               4._____
5._____               6._____
Ways to make nine starting with 5
1._____               2._____
3._____               4._____
5._____               6._____
Ways to make nine starting with 10
1._____               2._____
3._____               4._____
5._____               6._____
An interesting thing I have discovered
_____
_____
_____
_____
```

As she worked through the programme, written evidence of Emily's use of standard triples during the non-calculator phase tended to decline. It became noticeable that for the first four numerals in her sequence, 9, 7, 8, and 6 she gave at most two, but then she provided other 'non standard', combinations. When working with 7, for example, she provided 10 + 10 + 10 - 20 - 3; with eight she provided 99 - 91 and 34 - 32 + 6. Working with the calculator she provided written evidence of combinations such as 90 - 80 - 4 = 6, 2 + 9 + 1 - 6 = 6, 30 - 15 - 9 = 6, 40 - 30 - 5 = 5, 10 + 30 - 30 - 2 = 8, 5 + 20 - 19 = 6.

It soon became evident that Emily's understanding of the relationships between numbers was beginning to change. She began to see a different framework for working with numbers:

Well,... before I would have found it harder with nine, but ... um ... its not that hard because I know that ten is really easy so nine is really easy because you just take away one from ten ...

It was easier to take away from eight than I thought it would be. Before I found it a bit hard with the other number. I thought eight would be a bit hard. But in the end it wasn't as hard as I thought it would be.
I have discovered it is much easier to use multiplication in sums.

Inevitably pattern became a feature of Emily's discovery and it was common for Emily's written work to include extensive use of any numbers up to 100. At times she included numbers over 100 in her combinations. She was beginning to realise that:

It is a lot easier to work with big numbers than I thought ... I thought that big numbers would be very hard because they are so big ... but it isn't. It is just the same as low numbers.

It was evident from our discussions that Emily was now talking about numbers as objects. During all of the interviews that followed work with the calculator, only on one occasion did she volunteer information about her dots. However it was not until a series of follow-up interviews in January 1996 that we began to obtain some evidence that her imagery may be changing. When asked to think about numbers that make seven, Emily's first comment was:

I just see the symbol 7 flashing in my mind waiting, as if I was about to add it up ...

During our investigations into children's imagery, no other low achiever had associated the word 'flashing' with symbolism to describe imagery. The word had dominated descriptions of imagery by high achievers. Other numbers were also associated with this notion of flashing and when directly asked to talk about what she could see when she heard the word 'four' Emily responded by saying

4 flashes through my mind, and then I see, two twos like on a dice, 2 + 2, 100 - 96, four pounds ...

Discussion

In contrast to interaction with concrete objects which requires the individual to interpret what is going on, interaction with the supercalculator offers a system in which the individual could build and test concepts, first by observing and then by predicting and testing what happens. The form of presentation could be directly controlled by the child. What was becoming clear from our interactions with Emily was that she was building a different range of meanings associated with numbers and numerical symbolism - she was beginning to build a new image, a symbolic one that could stand on its own or be part of the options that would give flexibility. It seems as if her imagery was beginning to be associated with the notion of 'thought generator', rather than being seen as essential to thought.

Supercalculators can carry out the evaluation of numerical expressions whilst the child is concentrating on the meaning of symbolism that remains visible throughout. If arithmetical activity focuses on the process of evaluation and the meaning of the symbolism it can offer a way into arithmetic that helps those children who are experiencing difficulty develop a more powerful understanding of symbols.
However, belated emphasis on the ambiguous meaning of symbolism, when the greater proportion of previous experience has emphasised procedural and manipulative aspects, is embraced with difficulty. There may be a need to reappraise the emphasis on counting procedures with 'low achievers'. It may be too late once the die is cast.

References

1. E.M.Gray & D.O.Tall: *Success and failure in mathematics: the flexible meaning of symbols as process and concept*, MTI42, 1993, pp6-10
2. Ruthven: 'Developing algebra with a supercalculator', *Micromath*, 9, 1993, pp 23-25

Eddie Gray and Demetra Pitta work at the University of Warwick Mathematics Education Research Centre

Meindert Beishuizen describes mental models and pencil-and-paper models for supporting mental calculation.

MENTAL ARITHMETIC: MENTAL RECALL OR MENTAL STRATEGIES?

One of the arguments for developing mental arithmetic is that dealing with numbers in a holistic way makes numbers and number operations more meaningful than carrying out the standard tens and units algorithms [1]. More recently, the value of flexible cognitive strategies in mathematical problem solving has been recognised, and informal non-standard strategies are believed to stimulate such flexible thinking. In the UK, the Calculator-Aware Number (CAN) project advocated a radical shift towards such an approach and promoted calculators and informal mental methods in schools instead of written algorithms [2].

In the Netherlands, written column arithmetic is not introduced until Year 4 (Groep 5) in Dutch maths textbooks. In our country, as in Germany, there is a long tradition of emphasising mental arithmetic in the lower grades. One of the purposes of this article is to describe a model designed to improve flexibility of mental computation, which we call the 'empty number line' [3]. This model was recently introduced within the Realistic Mathematics Education (RME) project at Leiden University, where we developed an experimental number-line program. We have evaluated this approach with ten Year 3 (Groep 4) classes (N=275), in co-operation with the Freudenthal Institute [4].

Leiden on Sea

Figure 1 shows how three pupils - Wilco, Eddy and Brit - set about the solution of the problem *Leiden on Sea*. The problem context is designed to suggest an informal 'Adding-on-to' solution strategy, bridging the gap between the two numbers.

Wilco's solution follows the given problem structure closely, and is strongly

supported by the number-line model and the decade landmarks 10, 20, 30 between 9 and 31. (We label this **tens-to-tens** step procedure *A10*). Notice, however, that the number line is an empty line; the pupils themselves make decisions whether and where to position and draw marks, numbers, etc. Wilco did so rather carefully, to support his solution. However, it is not only this modelling function, but also mental imagery and mental activation, which makes the empty number line a more powerful teaching approach than recourse to the popular tens and units apparatus, or even the more abstract hundred square that we have used in the past.

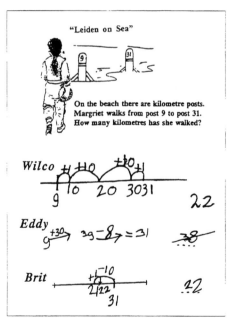

Fig 1.

In the first part of our teaching programme, pupils start working on a pre-structured number line with marks for the tens, in order to become familiar with the model. They also learn the new mental procedure of **jumping by ten** from any number (we label this procedure *N10*). A **compensation** procedure (*N10C*) - such as [add 9] via [add 10, subtract 1] - fits very well into this sequential development of number and problem representation. Eddy *(Fig1)* uses a minimal representation of the number line and a form of compensation (though not entirely successfully in this instance). In the third solution of Brit, a more able pupil, we see how this pre-knowledge can be used in a flexible way. She is not bound by the given problem structure, but imposes a transformation to a subtraction strategy [31 - 9] to solve the problem, and a compensation procedure [31 - 10 + 1] to achieve an elegant shortcut solution.

Mental arithmetic and SATs

SCAA [5] has recently published some sample materials to enable schools to practise for a Key Stage 2 pilot test on Mental Arithmetic, to be administered in May 1997. The manual says that the test 'is designed to assess children's mental recall and agility when dealing with numerical problems'. Children are not allowed to do written working, and have to respond within time limits of 5, 10 or 15 seconds to the orally presented questions. 'The shorter questions involve single calculations which are based on knowledge (recall), while the longer response questions involve more complex calculations.' *Figure 2* shows some sample test questions.

(5 sec.)	Write the number that is six less than one hundred.
(5 sec.)	What is three point two multiplied by one hundred?
(15 sec.)	What is the cost of four video tapes at two pounds ninety-nine pence each?
(15 sec.)	One eighth of a number is two point five. What is the number?

Fig 2.

Some of the longer questions implicitly offer the possibility of using mental strategies like rounding up and compensation, for example when working with £2.99. However, in most questions the emphasis is on mental recall and (complex) mental calculation in the head. This is in line with the teachers' manual, and is reinforced by the instruction that pupils are not allowed access to paper for working out answers. Other SCAA publications give the impression that informal mental strategies are not valued as highly as in other countries. For instance, the report on the 1995 Key Stage 2 tests [6] points to the 'wide range of methods, including both standard and non-standard approaches, employed by children.' The reports advocates 'a balance' in teaching between encouraging children to develop 'own methods' and providing them 'straightforward and efficient standard methods'. The report gives some examples to illustrate that children's own non-standard mediods for solving number problems in the collected test materials 'were often inefficient and time-consuming' *(Figure 3)*.

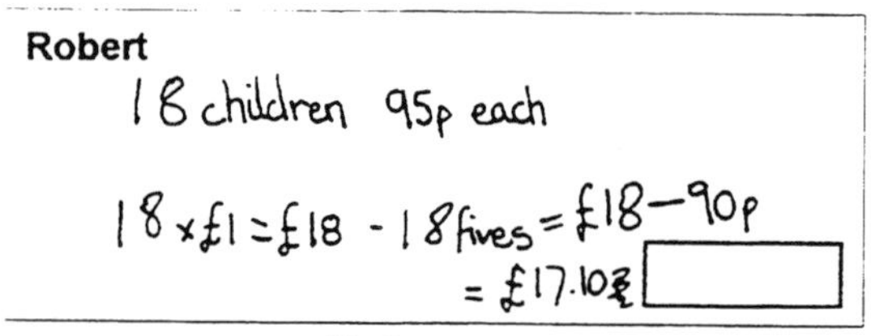

Robert

18 children 95p each

$18 \times £1 = £18 - 18\text{ fives} = £18 - 90p$
$= £17.10$

Fig 3.

From a Dutch point of view, however, the method used in the given example would not be considered as inefficient; on the contrary it could be regarded as sensible use of a mental compensation strategy. It is true that, in the beginning, non-standard methods can be time-consuming; but if the learners are allowed to develop them further, they become more curtailed and more efficient. This 'progressive mathematization' argument is at the heart of RME-theory [3]. Such views are now widely accepted in mathematics education; engaging first with children's informal strategies, elaborating on them later, and moving towards more formal standard procedures. This is a much better learning trajectory than the other way round.

Surprisingly, this does not seem to be the view held by SCAA with respect to National Curriculum Mathematics. In any case, suggesting a contrast and advising 'a balance' between non-standard and standard methods, as SCAA [6] does, sounds very impracticable and unproductive. The Dutch hold a broader view of mental arithmetic, as we now set out to explain.

Defining and stimulating mental arithmetic

The post-Cockcroft period in the UK witnessed a revival of mental arithmetic. At the same time, in the Netherlands, Dutch schools TV developed several innovative maths series for primary schools in conjunction with the Freudenthal Institute. One of these was dedicated entirely to encouraging mental arithmetic in the upper grades (Year 6, Groep 7). A six-month series contained pupils' worksheets, a teachers' manual for classroom discussion of different strategies - as well as a TV quiz competition on mental arithmetic between school teams! The series was broadcast between 1986 and 1988, and more than 1000 primary schools participated. One article on the evaluation study was published in the UK [7].

In fact, mental arithmetic was not very popular in the Netherlands in the early 1980s, because it had a traditional flavour associated with rehearsal of basic number facts, times tables, and so on. Nevertheless, as *Figure 4* shows, the school TV series did emphasise knowledge of number facts alongside the development of flexible mental strategies and estimation. In comparison, the SCAA test *[Fig2]* is much more narrow in its view of what mental arithmetic entails.

It is salutary to note that in the Netherlands, during the 1980s, there was a popular belief that 'discovering' number relations was more important than knowing number facts, and that emphasis on mental strategies would necessarily strengthen basic number - without any additional training.

That viewpoint was too optimistic, however, and was not confirmed by research. Efforts to achieve a more balanced view on mental arithmetic - as expressed in the school TV series - became a focal point of Dutch discussion. The distinction made above was crystallised among teachers and students in two expressions: doing mental arithmetic *in your head* (number facts) and doing mental arithmetic *with your head* (mental strategies).

In the latter case, written working is allowed and even encouraged by providing 'scrap-paper' boxes on the test form. Having children record the steps of their mental solutions is another (metacognitive) aspect of the modern 'strategies' argument [8]. Use of this is becoming more widespread now in the Netherlands, and the empty number line is a very good model for this purpose (Figure 5]. Similar boxes for 'working out' are provided in the written SATs for England and Wales at KS1 and KS2, as well as a variety of realistic and formal problems. Why then does SCAA hold to such a restricted view on non-standard methods and mental arithmetic? As I remarked earlier, in Dutch eyes this viewpoint is difficult to understand (although SCAA has recently published a discussion paper with a wider view on mental arithmetic) [9].

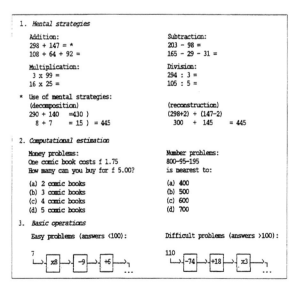

Fig 4.

The empty number-line programme

These discussions in the 1980s led to a re-thinking in our country, not only of mental arithmetic, but also of basic number teaching up to 20 and up to 100. Empirical studies have enabled us to codify and systematise the teaching of mental arithmetic strategies and procedures (such as N10 and so on). Re-invention of the 'arithmetic rack' and the 'empty number line' were important outcomes [3]. The new models were designed to serve both basic number operations and flexible mental strategies. The latter 'strategies' aspects often get more attention in the literature, but basic number facts are also important; indeed, they were re-discovered as indispensable prerequisites for flexible use of mental strategies.

Therefore *the first part* of the empty number-line programme pays much attention to such basic aspects as number concept, number operations (N10-jumps), and number facts like splitting up the units (eg. knowing that 7 is 2+5 when adding 7 to 48). During this first part, operations on units, using problems such as 48+7 and 84-9, are emphasised and practised on the empty number line. Unit-splitting and number relations like 9 + 1 = 10 (and so 9=10-1) get a lot of attention, because knowing them as automated number facts is a prerequisite for flexible shortcut strategies - as we saw earlier in the Leiden on Sea problem *(Fig1)*.

Mental strategies are much more central in *the second part* of the program. In *Figure 5*, we see the answers of two 'weaker' pupils, indicating two different kinds of development.

Wilco continues to use the support of the (empty) number-line model for safety as he did before *(Fig 1)*, although he now demonstrates *(Fig 5)* the use of the more sophisticated compensation strategies. Eddy, having previously been rather casual about drawing his jumps, now prefers to quit the number line altogether and just writes down his mental steps. He had started trailing compensation strategies *(Fig1)* earlier; Eddy now successfully uses both standard N10 and his own curtailed variant of A10 *(Fig 5)*. He demonstrates flexible use of mental strategies - showing that there is life beyond the empty number line.

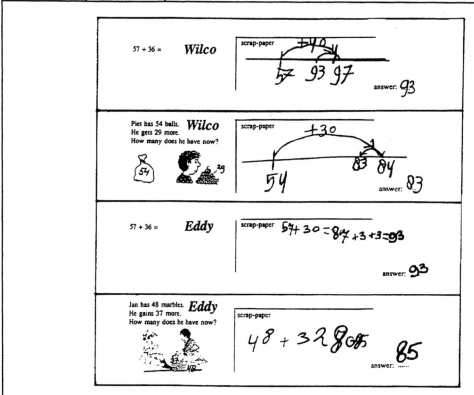

Fig 5.

References

1. S Plunkett: 'Decomposition and all that rot', *Mathematics in School* 8 (3), 1979, pp. 2-5.
2. T Rowland: 'CAN in Suffolk: the first six months of a calculator-aware number curriculum (second edition)', Homerton Research Reports Series, Cambridge, Publication Unit, Homerton College Cambridge, 1994.
3. A Treffers: 'Didactical background of a mathematics program for primary education', in L Streefland (Ed.), *Realistic mathematics education in primary school*, pp.21-56, Utrecht: Freudenthal Institute, 1991.
4. T Klein, M Beishuizen & A Treffers: 'The empty number line in Dutch second grades under two conditions: a Realistic versus Gradual program design', paper at the European Research Conference on the Psychology of Mathematics Education (ERCME), Osnabruck, Germany, 1995.
5. SCAA: *Mathematics Key Stage 2 - Mental arithmetic - sample test materials*, London: SCAA, KS2/97/688, 1997.
6. SCAA: *Report on the 1995 Key Stage 2 tests and tasks in English, Mathematics and Science*, London: SCAA, KS2/95/340,1995.
7. M Beishuizen & K van Putten: 'The use of videotaped broadcasts in interactive teaching', *British Journal of Educational Technology*, 21, 1990, pp. 95-105.
8. M van den Heuvel-Panhuizen & K P E Gravemeijer (1991): 'Tests are not all bad - An attempt to change the appearance of written tests in mathematics instruction at primary school level', in L Streefland (Ed.), *Realistic mathematics education in primary school*, Utrecht: Freudenthal Institute, 1991, pp. 139-145.
9. SCAA: *The teaching and assessment of number at Key Stages 1-3*, Discussion Paper No 10, London: SCAA Ma/97/762,1997

Meindert Beishuizen teaches at Leiden University in the Netherlands. This article was written whilst he was a Visiting Scholar at Homerton College, Cambridge. Tim Rowland provided assistance with the English version of the article

Kevin Holloway describes how a group of primary teachers have been exploring for themselves some of the issues around mental arithmetic in the primary school.

EXPLORING MENTAL ARITHMETIC

For six months now I have been working with a group of teachers who come from four schools in and around the Dewsbury area, exploring the issue of mental arithmetic by sharing their practice. At each monthly meeting we describe and discuss developments since the previous meeting and jointly decide on a fresh focus for the next period of classroom work, so that discussion and classroom activity have, to a large extent, been based on the group's own experiences. Between the meetings individuals have kept journals, detailing the work followed through in the classroom, together with comments and observations on the outcomes.

Recently I reviewed the progress we have made so far, looking at notes from meetings and reading comments in teacher's journals. A number of themes became apparent:

- strategies (children's),
- mental images,
- links between mental approaches and written methods,
- self-esteem issues,
- implications for teaching and beaming mathematics.

Strategies

By strategies I mean those techniques we come to use automatically for calculating mentally (sometimes they are taught to us, sometimes we seem to invent them ourselves). Doubling and halving is one strategy: we might know that 15 + 16 is 31 because we know that 15 doubled is 30 and one more is 31. Using number bonds to partition numbers is another: 27 + 8 is 35 because 27 + 3 is 30 and 30+5 is 35. We know that children's mental strategies can be very sophisticated. This is David's (Y6) written version of what he thinks he does in his head:

	572-394
1.	300 - 500=200
2.	70 - 90= 20
3.	20 - 200= 180
4.	2 - 4= 2
5.	2 - 180= 178

Interestingly, children's strategies were not what first came to mind for many of the teachers in the group at our first meeting. There was a general view that mental arithmetic was simply a loosening-up activity at the beginning and end of mathematics sessions - a valuable add on. So we went away from the first meeting to try a range of activities suggested by members of the group. One of the first tentative comments in our next meeting, however, was: "it's not just getting them to do it, it's making sense of what's going on in their heads". This became our next focus and teachers encouraged children to make their own personal strategies clear to the teacher and to each other:

Through talking to the children I now know that Y6 children employ a variety of strategies, (some weird and wonderful). Many Y6 children are not confident and need the benefit of other children's thoughts and processes.
Project teacher.

Having found that many children do have clear strategies which they seem to have developed themselves the question has now been asked: can we teach these in an organised way? In part, I think the answer is yes: anyone who works orally with a group of children who have been encouraged to use a particular strategy, doubling and halving, for example, will notice a difference between their responses and those of a group who have not done that work. But which strategies should we teach and what progression should there be? For me warning lights flash at the notion of one progression suiting all children.

I do try to teach some strategies but am well aware that the children in my maths set do generally have quite good strategies - things that work well for them - and I don't really see a need to change that. I think there is a danger of showing too many methods.
Project teacher.

We need to understand more clearly the building blocks which will allow children to construct their own approaches, these include:

- number bonds, understood and learnt as facts, which extend up the number line as far as possible,
- multiplication facts, understood and learnt,
- a ready ability to double and half,
- mental images of the number line, with a sense of counting in tens and hundreds, not just ones.

Other mental images

What can children be encouraged to 'see' which would be helpful? One important issue which has begun to be discussed in the group is the usefulness, or otherwise, of structural apparatus like base-10 Dienes materials. It has been suggested [see, for example, 1] that breaking numbers apart in the way that base ten materials do might not be as helpful as has been thought and it has been fascinating to see members of our group beginning to have similar doubts quite independently. Teachers are feeling that describing and showing with blocks the number 341, for example, focuses too much on the individual digits and gives no real sense of the number, particularly if this is also done without the context of a number line.

The arrow cards which the Wakefield numeracy project has been using are a valuable alternative approach to understanding numbers.

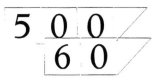

Related to this is a growing tendency among the group to give children any number calculations in a horizontal form - *'horizontal format in, vertical out'* wrote one teacher. This seems, she said, to allow her children to appreciate the value of the numbers and gives them a choice about how they then deal with them.

Links between mental approaches and written methods

Increasingly, teachers in the group are pointing out how children's mental strategies and written versions of mental strategies are very different from the standard algorithms and are based on very different understandings of number:

I realise that I come from a very formal mathematical background and have relied until now on the translation of this into teaching methods. However, having seen the variety of methods utilised by children, it's apparent that the mental approach to maths is almost diametrically opposed to the written contentions.

Project teacher

So how do we relate mental and written forms of mental strategies to the 'written conventions'?
Perhaps we should simply find ways of helping children make the approaches they have devised and understand more efficient. There is, however, a very strong lobby for a formal teaching of the standard algorithms from an early stage. Is it possible to marry the encouragement of children's own written methods to the teaching of standard algorithms? We shall soon be able to see something of what can happen when this is attempted through the work of the *National Numeracy Project*.

Their *Framework for Numeracy* includes this statement:

"Pupils should be taught to develop and refine pencil and paper methods for calculations (+ and -) building on mental methods."

There are several interesting points here. One is that examples of work in the *Framework for Numeracy* are almost always presented in a vertical form and, where horizontal presentation is suggested, it is clearly expected that children will rearrange the numbers and work vertically. Presumably, this is because the work is seen as leading to standard algorithms. As I have indicated earlier, a number of the teachers in our group have found that a horizontal presentation helps the children deal with the numbers with understanding: a vertical presentation sometimes seems to prevent understanding. A second point relates to the implied element of progression in the examples. Clearly, these written versions of mental processes are seen as a step on the road to the standard algorithms as a destination. To any person, child or adult, who understands number and how to work with it mentally, the standard algorithms, when eventually met, can make sense and may be seen as handy tools, as efficient and concise techniques, but they are not goals in themselves. The *National Numeracy Project's Framework* document seems to have much in it that is very positive, not least the idea that mathematics in the primary school needs to be taught. It will be interesting to see how the project eventually deals with the relationship between mental arithmetic, written forms of mental approaches and standard methods.

Self-esteem

This has been, for me, an unexpectedly important feature of the work. A number of teachers in the group have observed how their children, after initially feeling rather threatened by whole-class mental arithmetic and discussion of the methods they use, responded very positively:

I am pleased with how children now see numbers as far more of a 'fun' thing because there is more talk between the children. Debates spontaneously occur as children try to help others understand their way of doing things, and as they discuss which ways are more efficient.

... far more of my teaching has not required a written answer. Children have felt freer to express themselves in a confident and accurate way because the format has not been questioned.

After seeing the children's confidence with numbers increase and the actual amount of work which can be covered orally I am beginning to devote more and more time to mental work and strategies Whole class work has its obvious problems but it does encourage children of less ability when they see others so confident with numbers

Project teachers.

It is exciting to see children clearly enjoying themselves with number.

Implications for teaching and learning mathematics

Teachers in the group have clearly enjoyed working with their classes or groups in an interactive and focused way. They have been planning for and managing the work; not simply distributing text books or work books and hoping that the children's solo progress through the pages will result in learning. Too many children spend their primary school mathematics lessons never talking about mathematics or hearing mathematics talked about. But the teachers in this group are addressing issues with their children and enjoying the interaction and quality of learning which results. They are actually focusing the teaching and learning going on in the classroom rather than leaving the children to make what sense they can of sets of commercial materials.

This group has already addressed more questions than we could ever have thought of when we started out. I think we can anticipate many more.

With thanks to teachers and children from Bywell Junior School, Field Lane JI and N School, Headfield Junior School, Hyrstmount Junior School, Staincliffe Junior School and other colleagues from Kirklees LEA.

Reference

1. A Wigley: Teaching Number, a radical re-appraisal, MT146

Kevin Holloway teaches at University College, Bretton Hall, West Bretton, Wakefield.

Mike Askew looks at what is involved in calculating in your head.

MENTAL METHODS OF COMPUTATION

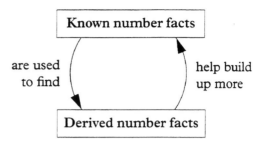

I want to suggest that there are two distinct aspects of mental computation, each of which has to be worked on explicitly with children. First there are mental methods of computation that are based on either instant or rapid recall of number facts. Having a repertoire of number facts, such as number bonds to 10 + 10 and multiplication facts to 10 x 10, is part of having a sound foundation in number. It is this aspect of mental computation that the traditional mental arithmetic tests tended to focus on.

The second aspect of mental mathematics that also has to be addressed is the ability of children to figure out mentally number calculations that they cannot rapidly recall. For example, it is unlikely that anyone would commit to memory the answer to 46+58, but children who are confident in number are able to find the answer mentally.

Research suggests that these two aspects of mental mathematics - knowledge of number facts and strategic methods - appear to be complementary [1, 2]. Studies of arithmetical methods used by seven- to twelve-year-olds demonstrate that higher attaining pupils are able to use known number facts to figure out other number facts. For example, a pupil may 'know by heart' that 5 + 5 = 10 and use this to 'figure out' that 5 + 6 must be eleven, one more than 5 + 5. At a later stage, a pupil may know that 4 x 25 is 100 and use that to figure out that 40 x 24 must be 960.

The evidence suggests that pupils who are able to make these links between recalled and deduced number facts make good progress, because each approach supports the other.

Eventually, some number facts that pupils previously deduced become known number facts and, in turn, as their range of known number facts expands so too does the range of strategies that they have available for deriving facts.

However, it is also clear that there are many children who, even by the end of primary school, rely more on procedures such as counting to find the answer to calculation and do not make as much progress. It is therefore important to work on strategic methods even in Key Stage 1 and not leave children using counting methods beyond the point at which they might develop more efficient methods.

At Key Stage 1 what number facts might we expect children to know, and what might we expect them to be able to deduce? At a minimum, I would suggest that children might be expected to be able to do the following by instant or rapid recall:

- add and subtract one from any number to 10;
- add 10 to any single digit number;
- know the complements to 10: the pairs of numbers that add to 10: 2 + 8, 3 + 7 etc;
- know the doubles to 10 + 10;
- use the commutative law 2+8 = 8+2.

Strategies that Key Stage 1 children might use to deduce number facts up to 20 include the following:

- use the known double facts to rapidly find near doubles, for example 6 + 7 is one more than 6 + 6;
- rearrange the order of calculation, for example given 8+13, calculate 13+8;
- rearrange the numbers, for example appreciate that 18 + 3 will give the same result as 13 + 8;
- add or subtract 9 by adding or subtracting 1 0 and adjusting the answer by 1;
- bridge through 10, for example calculating 8+6 as 8+2+4.

In Key Stage 2, assuming children are confident with the addition and subtraction bonds to 20, further strategies that they might use to help them mentally to add any two 2-digit numbers include:

- partitioning both numbers into their component tens and ones, adding the tens, adding the ones and adding the two totals together, for example finding the answer to 38+27 by adding 30 and 20 to get 50, 8 and 7 to get 15 and finally adding the 50 and 15 to get 65;
- keeping one number intact and partitioning the other number into its component tens and ones, adding the tens to the intact number and then adding the ones - finding the answer to 38+27 using this method would mean adding 20 to 38 to get 58 and then adding on the 7 to get 65;
- rounding one number to a multiple of 10 and either adjusting the second number or adjusting the answer - so 38+27 could be calculated by saying that this is the equivalent of 40+25 (rounding the 38 up to 40 and compensating for this by reducing the 27 by 2) or adding 40 and 27 to get 67 and then subtracting the 2.

Which method children use for addition of two two-digit numbers may affect their ability to extend this into carrying out subtractions mentally. The method that involves partitioning both numbers into their component tens and ones can be thought of as a ten-ten (TT) method. The method that involves keeping one number

intact, and partitioning the other number into its component tens and ones can be thought of as a number-ten (NT) method. Research suggests that children who use the NT method find it easier to adapt this to subtraction problems than children who use the TT method [3].

All the above suggests that at any time a particular child will be at three different levels of mental mathematics: she will have a bank of 'known facts', a bank of number facts that she can figure out (which may or may not eventually become known facts) and a range of strategies for deriving facts.

This raises questions about how best to manage mental arithmetic sessions so that as many children as possible are fully engaged. The traditional method of asking a question and waiting for the volley of hands to go up does have several drawbacks, particularly in emphasising the rapid, the known, over the derived - those children who 'know' the answer invariably beat those who still have to figure it out.

The trick for the teacher is to find ways to provide some thinking time (but not an endless amount). Strategies that are successful include insisting that nobody puts a hand up until the teacher gives the signal and silently counting to five or ten before giving the signal or insisting that everybody keeps as still as possible, that not even by raising an eyebrow should anyone indicate that they think they have the answer.

References

1. E M Gray: *An analysis of diverging approaches to simple arithmetic: preference and its consequences, Educational Studies in Mathematics*, 22(6), 1991, pp. 551-574.
2. L P Steffe: *Children's algorithms as schemes, Educational Studies in Mathematics*, 14, 10, 1983.
3. M Beishuizen: 'New research into mental arithmetic strategies with two-digit numbers up to 100', in *European conference on educational research*, University of Bath, 1995.

Mike Askew teaches in the School of Education at King's College, London

Section 3:
Issues and Examples
from the Classroom

This design is taken from the ATM Activity Pack - Holes
The pack contains 16 full colour cards illustrating holes from the environment,
plus photographs of computer generated images

Holes pack prepared by Lyndon Baker and Ian Harris

SECTION 3:
Issues and Examples from the Classroom

In the previous sections the main focus has been upon why and how we teach and children learn mathematics. There are many issues here for us all that challenge our assumptions and our practice.

To make sense of all the research and advice, to evaluate it, reflect upon it and to see how we could change our own practice, we need to take a good look at how the ideas are brought to life in classrooms. This section offers windows onto such classroom action, and with them the opportunity to reflect and re-consider.

We start with two activities that proved engaging and provided much diagnostic information. Exploring arithmogons, Diane Stoncel's year 3 class are captured building up positive attitudes to number work. The context allows them to explore patterns, solve problems using trial and improvement, and practice their number bonds. Pat Cannell's Year 3's are seen exploring target numbers up to 100 and so becoming proficient with the beginnings of place value, with the calculator present as an important aid to their learning.

The next two articles focus on patterns which are a vital part of the fascination of mathematics. Kate Harland found a storybook on which to base her approach to the foothills of multiplication. Her infants also used calculators and became fascinated by the numbers. Andrejs Dunkels worked with nine year olds on the many and varied patterns that arise in tables of numbers, including the multiplication table. His is a positive reminder that, when tackled in the right spirit of exploration, colouring can be a very productive activity.

The urge to try to solve a puzzle or a problem is also at the heart of our subject. Jeanette Harrison and the Cornwall Key stage 2 Task Group found a story context that contained a series of problems and presented it to classes in years 2, 4 and 5. As the three accounts are brought together, we can see how the children of all ages became absorbed in the challenge.

Using stories for mathematics is rightly a recurring theme in Mathematics Teaching, as Sue Saunders' short piece confirms. The fact that her children decide how the magic pot will function today is clearly an important element in its success.

Many of these activities involve children in much discussion with each other and with the teacher. For Jean Edwards' years 2 and 3 class this 'maths talk' was a main objective, and the potential of such activities to expand and enrich vocabulary is well analysed.

We end with two classes investigating numbers, where the accounts reveal very clearly how this kind of activity can contain all of the previous elements and moreover meet numeracy concerns. The activities are absorbing, diagnostic, involve patterns and lots of rich mathematical communication. Firstly, Joe Powderly's year five class found out why 6174 is a special number and then sought a five digit equivalent. Finally, Naomi Wells' year six class explore the possibilities when the answer must be 99, but the rest is up to you. It is well worth dwelling on her answers to her own question: **'but what did *I* learn?'**

INTRODUCTION

Adrian Pinel

Diane Stoncel has been experimenting with different ways of teaching number to children in Year 3.

HOW FAR CAN YOU GO?

I had been working on number bonds with five groups of children in Year 3 from my team. Although I had the advantage of having taught many of the children the previous year and so could build on their experiences, there were also some children I did not know so well. I was looking for an activity which would provide me with an opportunity to assess those children who were new to my class and which would also give the others a chance to use and apply the skills I felt they were developing. I therefore had all five groups working on arithmogons at different levels. First I started with numbers in the circles and the children could put in the answers in the squares.

For one group, that was as much as they could do as they found addition difficult. They made piles of cubes and added them, together, then checked their answers on the calculator. With those I felt had mastered this idea we moved on to where the answers were in two squares and the numbers in two circles.

From that, through trial and error and manipulating piles of cubes, the children could find the third number and the third answer. With my brightest group I moved on further still and gave them just the answers in the squares. For a while they used the blocks and moved them around until they managed, through trial and error, to find the numbers for the circles. I had expected them to try numbers randomly and while they retained some enthusiasm for this approach I allowed them to continue. They eventually began to tire of this. They kept forgetting which numbers they had tried, and so kept repeating them. I asked them if they could think of a way to stop trying numbers they had already used. One of them came up with the idea of writing these numbers down. The others agreed it was a good idea, but then found this problematic too.

They kept repeating numbers they had used because they were not in order, so it was still difficult to keep track of which numbers they had used and which they had not. I asked them if they could think of a better way of writing down the numbers. One of them reminded me of the time they did the 'story of ten'. "We found a good way of writing down the numbers, Miss. We wrote down 10 and 0, then 9 and 1, then 8 and 2. It was easy."

"Yes, that is a brilliant idea but could you do it for 16?"

"I think so", said Nicholas. He wrote down 16 + 0,then 15 + 1 as he spoke and said, "Yes, it's easy you just go 16 and 0, 15 and 1, 14 and 2, 13 and 3 and so on". He continued to write this down until he got to 0 + 16 as the others looked on and agreed it was a good idea because you could then cross off each pair as it was tried out. The blocks ceased to be used and mental arithmetic took over. Nicholas told us that you could not use 16 and 0, 15 and 1 or 14 and 2 because "there wouldn't be a nought in the circle" and the numbers had to be smaller than 14 in the top circle for it to make sense. Eventually, with more trial and error, the correct pair of numbers for 16 was found and the third circle filled in.

The children did several more of these using the same strategy, but I still felt I could move them on a bit more. I asked them if they could see any pattern in what they had done. They looked for a while, but were unable to suggest anything. I thought it might be easier to find a pattern if the numbers were smaller, so I put 1, 2 and 3 in the circles and we found the answers were 3, 4 and 5. This excited them, so they suggested we try 2, 3 and 4 expecting to get 4, 5 and 6, rather than the answers of 5, 6 and 7. We also tried 3, 4, 5 and 4, 5, 6.1 then asked them to add up the numbers in the circles and the numbers in

Diane Stoncel

the squares. The first one came to 6 and 12, the second to 9 and 18 and the third to 12 and 24. Suddenly Jonathan noticed something, "Look", he said, "I know 6 is half of 12, 50 is 9 half of 18?" Out came the calculators and yes, 9 was half of 18 and 12 was half of 24... Unfortunately we had to stop there, but we shall continue next lesson.

I felt I had learned so much about the children's developing skills in this short period. It proved to be an activity, which was worthwhile for all groups, even those who had used the triangles for simple addition.

Diane Stoncel teaches at Mereway Lower School, Northampton.

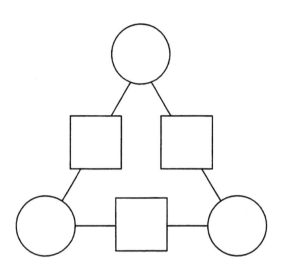

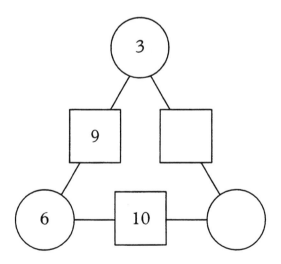

16
16 + 0
15 + 1
14 + 2
13 + 3
12 + 4
11 + 5
10 + 6
9 + 7
8 + 8
7 + 9
6 + 10
5 + 11
4 + 12
3 + 13
2 + 14
1 + 15
0 + 16

Name ___Jonathan___

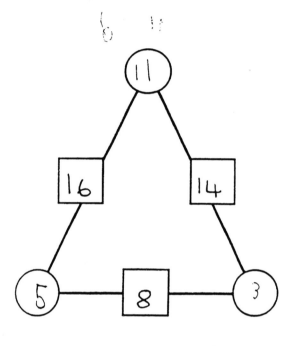

1, 2, 3

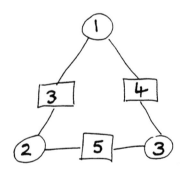

$+ O = 6$
$+ \Box = 12$ $= 18$

2, 3, 4

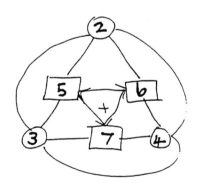

$+ O = 9$ $= 27$
$+ \Box = 18$

3, 4, 5

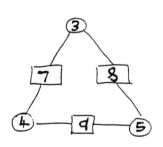

$+ O = 12$ $= 36$
$+ \Box = 24$

Diane Stoncel

What is place value? How can it be assessed, and where do calculators fit in?
Pat Cannell describes how the responses of year 3 children to an activity got her thinking.

IT AIN'T WHAT YOU DO -
IT'S THE WAY THAT YOU DO IT!

The original idea was to develop an activity that could provide calculator use in the classroom: an activity where the calculator could help develop strategies for the user by aiding number manipulation. I also wanted it to show me something of the children's understanding of place value. We had been doing a lot of work on place value and I found the level of understanding achieved difficult to assess. Most of my evidence came out in snippets of conversation. Maybe I could look at how the children used numbers in this activity and get an idea of what they had taken on board. A calculator is very quick at throwing up numbers. Do the children know the order of magnitude of those numbers?

The game was to find four numbers totalling a given target. Each target was arranged as shown. The outside squares were to be filled in to meet the target. I provided a work sheet with twelve such targets on, the first six being between 10 and 100, the latter six being all 100.

The class in question were Year 3, divided into three groups:
- Group 1 did the activity without a calculator or equipment. They could use scrap paper if they wanted to.
- Group 2 were given access to calculators but no direction.
- Group 3 were given a supply of squared paper.

The three groups did not carry out the activity simultaneously.

Within a few seconds of giving the first group their sheets I had to introduce some rules!

These were:
- No two numbers are to be the same.
- No noughts are to be used.

Group 1 set to and manipulated numbers with the aid of a rubber. They displayed a good grasp of place value, particularly with the repeated targets of 100, where they formed a strategy of building on the previous answer to make new totals.

Some of their solutions followed a pattern.

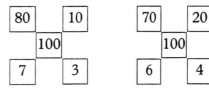

In some cases the strategy was handled better than the accuracy of the answers.

Group 2 were the lucky ones with the calculators, who thought they were well away, and so they pushed buttons and thought life was great. Then they got back to the task in hand and found that an initial strategy had to be formed manually. Mostly they picked a number then built up on it to meet the target. None of this group started at the total and worked backwards, which surprised me as that is how I would have gone about it!

After hitting the first couple of targets they added neither to found the calculator helpful but it added neither to their speed or their accuracy.

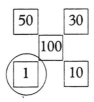

Chris's reasoning for this answer was *50 add 30 is 80, add 10 gets to 90 and 1 more ten gets me to 100.*

Group three were given the squared paper. This was my mistake. How easy, I thought, to count out the squares (I even gave them 100 squares), divide into four and then count each section. The children thought I was round the bend and proceeded in a way very similar to group 1. Some did use the 'apparatus' in the latter section, as can be seen from this example, where the number is broken down in a less convenient way.

I felt that the majority of the children showed a good grasp of place value, at least to 100, and they were developing strategies which involved breaking down the numbers into the largest working unit, in this case 'tens' and then shuffling those numbers about.

I also learnt that children's calculator use was not as effective as it might be - more activities required!

As a bonus there were some revealing results. Stephen completed the sheet in ten minutes without a calculator. As he was thirsting for more I quickly gave him a variety of, as I hoped, awkward numbers, a calculator and the instruction to get each number to zero in four moves. He did this very quickly by subtracting 100s, then 10s, splitting if necessary, and finally units.

$$1278 - 300 - 900 - 78 - 0 = 0$$

Neatly takes care of 1200

At the other extreme Sam showed a lack of understanding of the conservation of number. As he was obviously stuck on the first square I suggested that he used Multilink. On breaking a stick of 17 cubes

into two parts he was unable to say how many altogether. He also shows what a quandary he is in by the fact that one of his numbers around the edge is higher than the target.

Hayley, desperate to please and not be any trouble, dared not move far away from the target number, in case she lost her way; so the constituent numbers bear no relation to the exercise intended, but stay safely close to the target.

When this activity was tried with different older children a variety of more stringent rules were introduced, such as that no number may be divisible by 10.

When we were planning extensions the immediate thought was that large numbers would be difficult. We have now come to the opposite conclusion. If place value (upwards) is securely in place a large number presents no problem. However, consider 3 as the target number. This could take you in several directions according to the rules imposed:

* only integers can be used (negative numbers)
* parts of numbers can be used (fractions)
* all the numbers must be the same (interpreting a calculator display)

This has proved to be a versatile and revealing activity. My next task is to refine the targets and rules to make better use of a calculator.

Pat Cannell teaches at Southfield CP School, Brackley

Kate Harland has made good use of a storybook with her 5 & 6 year olds.

STARTING MULTIPLYING

Try to get hold of a copy of *Anno's mysterious multiplying jar* by Mitsumasa and Masaichiro Anno, (published by Bodley Head, but out of print at the time of writing) - I came across this book just by chance in the local children's library ... it looked fascinating and I wondered what my class of 5- and 6-year-old infants would make of it, as such we hadn't 'done' multiplying yet.

With a mixed group of nine children I started reading the story and the children drew as I read:

This is the story of one jar, and what was inside it.

In the jar there was water, which became ...

a vast great sea.

In the sea was 1 island ...

On the island there were 2 different countries ...

In each country there were 3 mountains ...

When I asked them simply: *how many mountains?* they answered '6' very quickly.

Some at this stage realised that they would need to redraw their pictures as they didn't have enough space:

And on each mountain there were 4 kingdoms ... We talked about what a kingdom was and they wanted to know how many there were. 24 was found by some children mentally, whilst others counted.

I wanted to leave the story there after this first half hour's work, but the group demanded to hear the rest

The next day

I decided to explore the story further with some calculators available. We only have sixteen calculators in the school and so the children haven't done much work using one. Again I provided them with paper for drawing. This time the children drew big islands.

1 island	1 on the calculator
2 countries	Some did 12, others 1 and 1 giving 11, some $1 + 1 = 2$ and others pressed clear and then 2.
3 mountains	How many mountains altogether? Some did $3 + 3 = 6$ and others I showed $2 \times 3 = 6$, for 2 islands x 3 mountains.
4 kingdoms	Ross Chard got 24 by counting first and then did 4+4+4 ... until he reached 24 on his calculator.

When I asked them about the five villages in each kingdom, Ross said that it was far too may to count, but Kai Hopkins, who had been listening hard, joined in:

20 villages on a mountain.

And on this mountain?

"20".

And this?

"20".

Kai and Ross together said: "there's 20 on every single mountain."

How many altogether?

Kai and Ross together again: "20 and 20 ... 40 ... another 20 ... 60 ... another 20 ... ... 120."

This was all done mentally which quite surprised me.

After that some tried the houses - 6 houses in each village.

I showed them the numbers in the second part of the book and they loved the 'thousands', but were disappointed that the dots stopped at the cupboard ... *(You'll have to get a copy of the book to understand that reference! - Eds)*

I continued to work with the book with small groups of children throughout the rest of the week. The last illustration shows Mark's (age 6) overall picture which he worked on later in the week. By then he was quite fluent with the calculator, although I helped him with the recording.

David Stokoe who teaches the top junior class in the same school read the book to his children and then asked them to draw it. They were fascinated that something that was all pictures in the first half could turn into numbers. Their drawings were more pictorial rather than representational, except for Henry's (see below).

In investigating the numbers the children were enthusiastic about their vastness.

It was good to find a story book which developed some mathematical ideas and could be used with children of different ages.

Does anyone know of other books which lend themselves to this sort of work?

Kate Harland teaches at Southville Primary School, Bristol

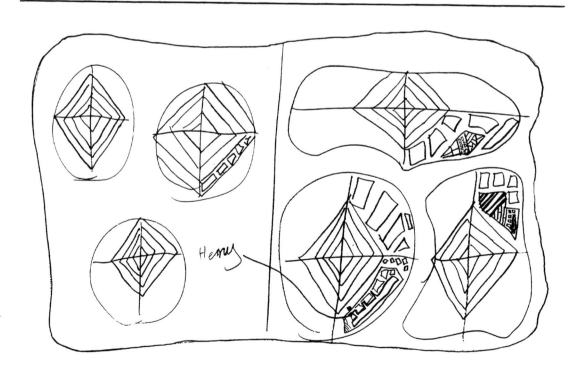

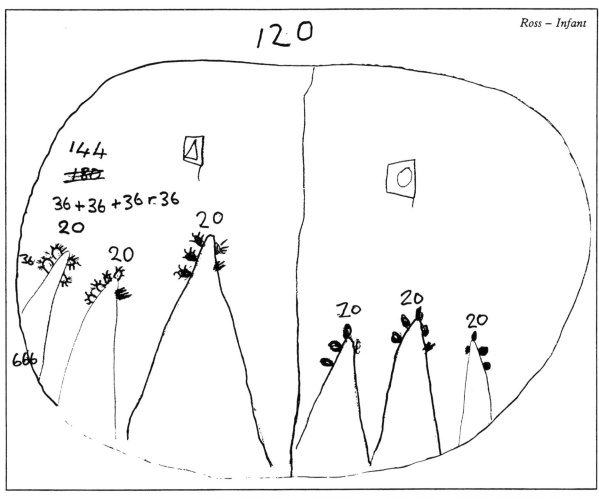

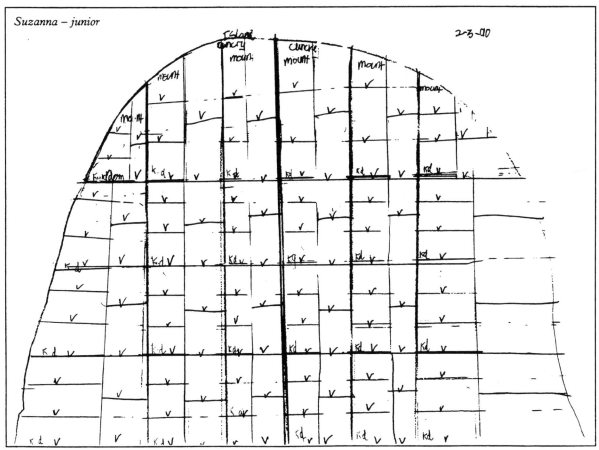

Kate Harland

Writing from Sweden, **Andrejs Dunkels** reminds us of the importance of looking carefully at the patterns and structures within some 'familiar' tables of numbers.

COLOURING THE MULTIPLICATION TABLE AND OTHER ARRAYS OF NUMBERS

The use of patterns in tables has been around in classrooms for a very long time all over the world, in certain countries more, in others less. So much has been written that it is impossible to make reference to every single article. A limited section, picked from my own bookshelf, is given in the last section.

Here 'tables' may mean addition tables, multiplication tables, the calendar for a particular month, hundred charts, and the like, that is, all kinds of arrays of numbers written according to some specified rule or system.

Since 1984 I have been conducting a teaching experiment on multiplication. Many fascinating events have occurred during the experiment and this article is meant to describe one of them.

Multiplication tables

Towards the end of the school year I wanted to review the multiplication facts in some interesting and thought provoking way with my class of 9 year olds. This naturally led to thinking about patterns, and I decided to try colouring the multiplication table, that is, colouring various subsets of the set of the 100 squares in a multiplication table 1 x 1 through 10 x 10. For that purpose I had produced many copies of such a table. All the worked out products were there in a 10 by 10 grid, as well as the 'headings' in the leftmost column and uppermost row.

x	1	2	3	4	5	6	7	8	9	10
1	1	2	3	4	5	6	7	8	9	10
2	2	4	6	8	10	12	14	16	18	20
3	3	6	9	12	15	18	21	24	27	30
4	4	8	12	16	20	24	28	32	36	40
5	5	10	15	20	25	30	25	40	45	50
6	6	12	18	24	30	36	42	48	54	60
7	7	14	21	28	35	42	49	56	63	70
8	8	16	24	32	40	48	56	64	72	80
9	9	18	27	36	45	54	63	72	81	90
10	10	20	30	40	50	60	70	80	90	100

Fig 1.

The figure shows the multiplication, or 'Pythagorean', table, with all the one hundred products worked out and displayed with headings in the leftmost column and the uppermost row.

By the way, the expression 'multiplication table' has at least two different meanings:

• First of all the expression may refer to 'the threes table', the fives table' or any specific sequence of products of the type 1 x n, 2 x n .... ,10 x n, or the other way round, n x 1, n x 2 ...., n x 10, which is then the n's table, where usually n is some number between 1 and 10. This interpretation of the expression is often generalised at some stage by allowing both factors to go beyond 10.

• Secondly the expression can stand for the set of all products from 1 x 1 through 10 x 10 worked out and arranged in order in a 10 by 10 square array. This table is sometimes called the Pythagorean table, although there is no historical evidence that Pythagoras ever used such a table.

Planning the pattern lesson

On the evening before the 'pattern lesson' I decided to try, as part of my planning and preparation, all activities I would let the pupils do. I wanted to start by reviewing the concepts of even and odd, and so the first activity would be to colour all squares containing an even number. I decided to use red first.

The activity was alright as far as colouring was concerned, I thought, as I worked with my sheet. In particular the emerging pattern was indeed pleasing. But the activity was not very fascinating from a mathematical learning or computational, point of view.

Andrejs Dunkels

What next, then? I would of course ask the children what an even number is, while they were busy with this activity. I would probably get the answer, 'A number that ends in 0, 2, 4, 6 or 8.' We could discuss the fact that that answer goes better with the question, 'How can we spot an even number among numbers written in our usual decimal place value notation?' I would remind the children that 'numbers don't actually care about how they are written or expressed', leading us to try a description, or definition, of even numbers without reference to the decimal notation. Somehow or other the discussion would eventually lead us to last digits, of course.

Therefore for our next activity, it would be natural to pick a digit and then colour all squares containing numbers ending in that particular digit.

I picked 4 and yellow as my first choices.

x	1	2	3	4	5	6	7	8	9	10
1	1	2	3	❁	5	6	7	8	9	10
2	2	❁	6	8	10	12	❁	16	18	20
3	3	6	9	12	15	18	21	❁	27	30
4	❁	8	12	16	20	❁	28	32	36	40
5	5	10	15	20	25	30	25	40	45	50
6	6	12	18	❁	30	36	42	48	❁	60
7	7	❁	21	28	35	42	49	56	63	70
8	8	16	❁	32	40	48	56	❁	72	80
9	9	18	27	36	45	❁	63	72	81	90
10	10	20	30	40	50	60	70	80	90	100

Fig 2.

The multiplication table with all those squares coloured where there is a number ending in a 4. In this figure colour has been indicated by the special symbol.
In actual practice the colour would usually not cover the digits completely, and so all the digits would be visible after the colouring.

Gradually a beautiful pattern emerged, and it was nice and pleasing. However, there had unfortunately been no mathematics going on while I coloured the squares, I felt. Of course patterns belong to mathematics, they form an important part, but it was too easy to spot all the numbers where the last digit was a 4. Everything was there in front of me, chewed and digested. Too much so, I felt.

I carried on. Now I chose a darker yellow, some would term it orange, and started colouring in the same table, all squares holding a number ending in a 6.

Again I felt the same as before: pleasing pattern, worthwhile as a pattern, but too little computation for my reviewing purposes.

Could I do something about the activity so that it would include more review of the actual multiplications? Could I change it somehow so that it included the computations as well as the pleasing patterns?

Empty table frames
How about the tables that I planned to distribute to the children? Perhaps each child would first of all have to fill in all the products. That would really involve a lot of multiplying. Of course, we had done this kind of thing several times before, and so that would then be review. But some children would be rather slow, and it would take some time before they got on to the colouring activity. And besides, that activity would be a repetition of an activity we had done before. I wanted something different. I knew that the children would like colouring.

But, I thought, do the tables I would distribute to the children have to contain any digits at all? The children would then enter the headings, and I would instruct them not to write any more numbers at all.

I tried for myself. I took a frame for a table, entered the headings, and said to myself, 'Now colour all those squares where there would have been a number ending in a 3, if all the numbers were actually written in the table.'

Andrejs Dunkels

This time there was quite a lot of computing going on as well as reasoning about the possibility of there being any more squares that had not yet been found and coloured. Although I do know all my multiplication facts, I had to think, I had to concentrate on the tables in quite a different way than before, when all numbers were explicitly there in front of me.

The pattern was at least as pleasing as before. In fact it was even easier, I thought, to spot the symmetry of the pattern, now that there were no digits there to obscure the view. I felt that I had found a way of including a pattern component as well as a computational component into the activity.

So the next morning I had to leave home early in order to make copies of empty table frames and leave the completed tables behind.

The table colouring that then followed was, if I may say so myself, a success.

No calculations whatsoever

The first activity was with the even numbers. The children started with a table frame, entered the headings, and started the colouring. It was fascinating to see how they gradually caught on to the idea that one can colour whole rows and columns. Towards the end of the colouring they were working fast, systematically, and energetically.

When we had discussed the even numbers activity leading to last digits, each pupil got a new empty table frame, and we carried on with the last digit 4. Then we continued with the last digit 6 in the same table, and I suggested that they could use another shade of the same colour, if they wanted to. Some of their work is shown at the end of this article.

When a table had been completed by colouring all squares where there would have been a number ending in a certain digit, the same table frame was used for all numbers ending in the ten complement of that digit.

Then another empty table frame would be taken and a new digit selected, and so, until all the combinations 4-6, 3-7, 2-8, 1-9 had been exhausted. We put 0 and 5 in the same table frame.

Each child worked at his or her own pace.

The children were surprised to find that there are so many symmetries in the multiplication table.

As they left the classroom after this lesson I heard some say to each other 'Today we've not done any calculations at all in the maths lesson, we have just been colouring all the time.'
Later some of them collected all the colouring in one single frame, a magnificent pattern.

Further work

Later we looked at the patterns with digits rather than colours. This was done, as usual, by first entering the headings and then filling each square with just the units digit of the actual product for that square. Again many children were surprised at the regularities.

x	1	2	3	4	5	6	7	8	9	10
1	1	2	3	4	5	6	7	8	9	0
2	2	4	6	8	0	2	4	6	8	0
3	3	6	9	2	5	8	1	4	7	0
4	4	8	2	6	0	4	8	2	6	0
5	5	0	5	0	5	0	5	0	5	0
6	6	2	8	4	0	6	2	8	4	0
7	7	4	1	8	5	2	9	6	3	0
8	8	6	4	2	0	8	6	4	2	0
9	9	8	7	6	5	4	3	2	1	0
10	0	0	0	0	0	0	0	0	0	0

Fig 3.

The multiplication table / Pythagorean table with just the units digits of the products displayed. Note the many symmetries and regularities. The nine's table is the reverse of the one's. Note also that there are always ten complements symmetrically around the column and the row of 0s and 5s of the fives table.

MT 136 SEPTEMBER 1991

Andrejs Dunkels

When I have performed these activities with teachers at in-service meetings many have said that they are surprised, and that they were not aware of all these symmetries. Most people know, and enjoy, the celebrated fact that the sequence of last digits of the numbers in the nines table is the reverse of the last digits of those in the ones table. But few are aware of the fact that the same applies to the eights and twos, the sevens and threes, and sixes and fours. But of course everybody knows that the fives has alternate 0s and 5s.

Later we did a similar activity with the tens digits; colour all the squares where there would be a number with the tens digit 3, and so on. This provided a nice review of the multiplication table from the viewpoint of the size of the numbers, 'which numbers in the thirties are in the multiplication table? In the sixties? The seventies?' And so on. The details of this are left to the reader and his or her pupils.

If some pupils show an interest in these activities then they can explore larger tables, up to 20 x 20 or even 30 x 30 or 40 x 40.

Tables within the table

It is also interesting to investigate other patterns, for example various multiplication tables within the multiplication table, that is, various sets of multiples of a given number within the Pythagorean table. This activity leads to question like, 'Does the sixes table go beyond 60?' We want the answer to this question to be affirmative, and so we must, at this stage, consider tables in the generalised sense.

Other natural questions are, 'Why is the pattern for the sixes table and the sevens so different?' -'Why do the patterns formed between the full rows and columns for the eights table contain five squares and for the nines just four?' These questions lead in a natural way to common factors and to prime numbers.

This activity is particularly well suited for 30 x 30 arrays or even larger ones.

The counting sequence

I have used the idea of empty frames with the counting sequence, which is often presented in a 10 by 10 array and referred to as a 100 chart.

I prefer to call it 'the counting sequence'. Then I am not restricted to any particular number of rows or any particular number of columns. I can start the sequence with 1 or 0, or in fact with any number I like.

At their first encounter with the counting sequence written in this particular way the pupils simply wrote it down and observed as many things as they could, and made notes of their observations.

After some time we skipped the written out numbers and looked at the squares alone, this time without any headings. We decided what number to start with in the uppermost left square, 0, say, and we decided how many squares there were to be in each row, and then gave tasks such as:

• Where will 14 be?

• Colour the square where 20 is.

• Colour all the squares where there would be a number ending in a 7.

• If I colour this particular square, where is the number that is 6 more than the number in the coloured square?

• Colour 15, 25, 35, 45, 55, and so on, as far as possible. - What numbers are in the same column?

• Can you find a rule for moving one step down along a column?

• Pick a starting number, 3, say, and colour that square. Then colour all the squares that you reach by successively adding 4.

When multiplication has been introduced the different multiplication tables can be viewed within this framework by colouring squares without any numbers written, except possibly for the starting number. To begin with I usually use 0 in the top left square and ten squares in each row when colouring multiplication tables. Later other starting numbers and number of squares in each row may be tried. It is particularly interesting to start with 2 and have 7 squares in each row and the following colouring rule:

Colour all multiplication tables, first the twos tables, then the threes, then the fours and so on. With one exception. If the first number of a particular table is not already coloured, then it should be left uncoloured. Use one colour only.

Questions:

* pick a coloured square. Why is it coloured?

* pick a non-coloured square. Why is it not coloured?

* repeat questions 1 and 2 several times.

* describe as precisely as you can the numbers whose squares are not coloured.

I leave the details of this to the reader and his or her pupils.

Concluding remarks

Patterns are important in mathematics and in the learning of mathematics. It takes time and effort on the part of the learner to get used to looking for patterns. One of my responsibilities as a teacher of mathematics is to provide my students with a variety of activities involving patterns.

Using empty frames for sets of numbers is one way that I have found useful, and that, as far as I can judge, enhances number sense and the feel for arithmetic. Empty frames also help the learner in his or her construction of knowledge about numbers. They enhance computation as well as pattern, which I find extremely useful. They help me to avoid the danger of the pattern activities becoming pattern alone.

Like any other new activity the first one with empty frames may seem difficult, too difficult in particular for the slow learner, one might feel. Thus the reaction might be that empty frames should be used with the able students only, as a special activity on Friday afternoon. My view is that empty frames are for all pupils. Empty frames provide an excellent opportunity for everybody, not least the slow learner, to think and reflect, as well as compute. The first empty frame activity must be preceded by work with complete tables, of course.

References

1. *Computation and Structure* (1967), Vol 2, Nuffield Mathematics Project, London
2. Dunkels, Andrejs (1989): *'What's the next number after G?'* The journal of mathematical behaviour Vol 8, No 1, pp 15-20
3. Henry, Boyd (1987): *Experiments with patterns in mathematics.* Dale Seymour Publications, Palo Alto
4. Howden, Hilde (1989): *Teaching number sense.* Arithmetic teacher, Vol 36, No 6, pp 6-11
5. *'One hundred things to do with a hundred square'* (1982), Mathematics Teaching, No. 100, pp 38-41
6. Litwiller, Bonnies H & Duncan, David R (1980): *Activities for the maintenance of computational skills and the discovery of patterns.* NCTM, Reston, Virginia.

Andrejs Dunkels was associate professor in the department of mathematics at the Lulea University of Technology, Sweden

Andrejs Dunkels, a long time member of the ATM sadly died during the production of this book.

Work from nine year old children of Ohemsskolan, Gammelstad and Porsoskolan, Lulea, Sweden

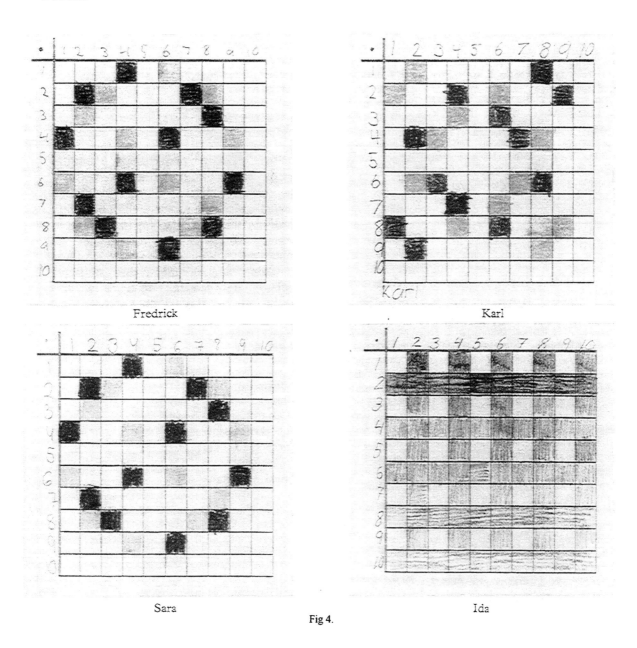

Fredrick

Karl

Sara

Ida

Fig 4.

Jeanette Harrison was introduced to a story by a colleague on a 20-day course, which could be used as a starting point for mathematical activity. She developed this for her colleagues at Threemilestone Junior & Infant School, Truro. The idea was written up by Cornwall's Key Stage 2 Task Group and this article is adapted from their work.

THE KING'S JEWELS

The King's Jewels

The King of Camelot owns some very precious jewels. However last week he had them stolen. There are 16 of them and you know where they are.

You go to fetch them but discover that you can only carry them back to the King on the MAGIC FLYING HORSE. Can you stick the jewels together so that they are strong and safe to carry back on the horse?

Now draw a PLAN of how you have stuck the jewels together. Now, because these jewels are so precious, if anyone sees you on the way back to The King they might try to attack you. What could you make to put the jewels in so that nobody can see them? ...A BOX!!! Can you draw a plan of how to make your box? Remember the jewels mustn't rattle about inside, or else they might break. Can you see if your box will work?

Planning the activity

Jeanette's Y2 class had enough Multilink cubes for each child to work with sixteen. They were available in several places around the room on group tables. Although the activity was presented for individuals to work at, discussion was encouraged to enhance the quality of what the children were doing and to avoid the negative aspects of competition. Jeanette worked with the whole class on this activity and predicted that the following areas of the National Curriculum content might be encountered:

- counting (Ma2/2a2)
- conservation of number
- 2D and 3D shape and their representation (Ma4/4a1)
- nets (Ma4/4a1)
- measuring
- volume (Ma4/4d2)

as well as the three strands of Ma1
- applications
- mathematical communication
- reasoning, logic and proof

Drawing the strong shape

There needs to be a selection of papers available (squared, triangle, various dotty paper, plain). *(Ma1 Applications)*. The definition of 'strong shape' is for the children to decide *(Ma1 Applications)*. There are useful questions to ask about why a child has decided that theirs is a 'strong shape'. (For some general guidance on questioning see: 'What questions could I ask'? in MT145). The drawing activity is related to PoS statement Ma4/4a1. The collection, making and drawing of the shape is likely to take about forty-five minutes to an hour including discussion with individuals, groups and the whole class.

Proving that there are sixteen jewels

The teacher asked the children if they could show her that there were definitely sixteen jewels in their strong shapes. The responses to this were oral *(Mal - Mathematical Communication, various levels)* and included number bond work (Ma2/2a2) and an awareness of 3 dimensions (Ma4/4a1). For example, children described the cubes they could see on the outside and reported that they knew there were other cubes which they couldn't see. This provided an opportunity for developing children's own language and introducing mathematical terms as appropriate.

Making the jewel box

The children now needed access to paper, card, scissors, glue and sellotape. In the Year 2 classroom there was a 'junk box' with a number of different cardboard packages - some children found it useful to dismantle these to help them see what the flat shape (net) looked like. The teacher asked them to make their net in paper first - this saved the more expensive cardboard resource but also gave them an easier medium for folding.

The variety of methods used by children was encouraged and gave some insight into the Mal level of the child. For example: some rolled the shape on the paper to obtain a net; others cut out the shape of each face and stuck them together with sellotape; (Ma4/4a1 & Ma4/4a3) others wrapped their jewels in paper, unconcerned about a net.

A Y4 class

The number of jewels was increased to twenty-five and also, the children could choose between cubes and Multilink triangular prisms. The teachers found that:

a) increasing the number of cubes does not necessarily extend the activity to higher levels but may actually complicate the issues.
b) the prisms provided a very motivating activity at the building stage but presented almost impossible challenges when constructing containers.

(Mal - Reasoning, Logic & Proof - various levels)

A Y5 class

The original 16-jewel story was presented with additional requirements of a plan and elevation of the 'strong' shape (using squared paper) Isometric paper was made available to draw a 2D representation of the shape. Although all classes used different colour 'jewels', year 5 were asked to include this in their drawings. On the following day these drawings were used for others to re-create the shape. In this group all three strands of Mal were evident at various levels.

After some brief guidance on how to join dots on a triangular lattice to portray three dimensional cubes, the excitement generated by these emerging pictures led them easily into making their own designs.

The experience of making nets in earlier years made the more complex task here accessible. Almost everyone was able to use flaps in making their nets.

Representing 3D as 2D (Ma4/6a) is only one aspect of this relationship. Making 3D shapes from 2D representations was a requirement for this class as they attempted to make 3D shapes from other children's 2D representations. There were three outcomes from this activity.

a) the 3D shape made was a correct interpretation of the 2D representation
b) the 2D representation was not sufficiently well produced to allow for a correct 3D shape
c) some children needed a lot of support to achieve a satisfactory 3D shape

The challenge kept the motivation going and offered the teacher both assessment and diagnostic opportunities.

Once the children had constructed their containers, they were asked to investigate how many jewels the King would have had in his crown if their 'strong shape' had been twice/ three times as large.

About half the class immediately decided that it would be 32 multilink and proceeded

Year 2 prove there are 16 Multilink

$8 + 8 = 16$

to build their shape- it wasn't long before they realised that their new shape didn't look like the old one. Others just started to build a larger shape, attempting to make it look like their original.

This latter approach caused a management problem as they rapidly ran out of cubes! This is the point where it became necessary to group the children. The enlargement activity is unwieldy with this number of cubes; work with smaller shapes makes it more likely that the children will make a connection between a shape and its enlargement.

The notion of doubling in 3D is a difficult concept and only a couple of children finished up with a shape using 128 cubes; the 32 solution generated much valuable discussion.

Cornwall's Key Stage Two Task Group consists of:
The Mathematics Advisory Team (Colin Banwell, Geoff Dunn, Jenny Nash, Helen Williams) Ken Davis (Primary Adviser), Philip Aldis (Tintagel Junior & Infant School), Richard Gambier (Tolcarne Junior School), and Paula Ross (Threemilestone Junior & Infant School, now Deputy Headteacher at Marlborough Junior & Infant School, Falmouth.)

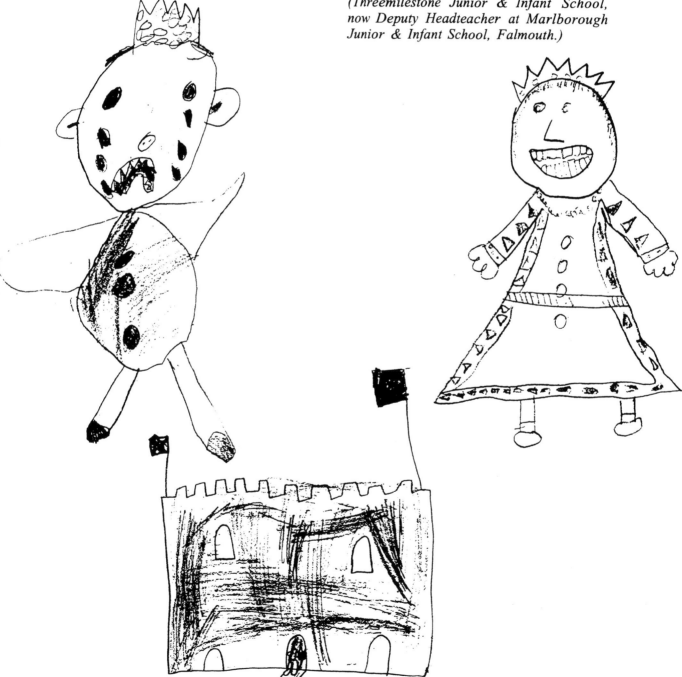

Sue Saunders responded to a question in *Mathematics Teaching*, giving her ideas about using stories, and a glimpse at how she approaches this.

MATHEMATICS AND STORIES

In *MT131* you asked if anyone has used reading material as a starting point for maths activities. I have used a particular story which may not have much merit as a piece of literature, but served a useful purpose as a launchpad for mathematics.

I first encountered this story when visiting my second year teaching practice school. I was listening to readers and this story comes from the *Through the rainbow* reading scheme, *Gold Book 4, Starlight and Sunshine* and is entitled *Mr and Mrs Goodbody* (pp78-93*). (A brief extract from the story is reproduced below - Ed).* I thought the idea of the magic pot would make a good maths activity, with the children imagining they had one into which they could put numbers.

I put the theory into practice and took in my mother's brass pot which looked quite effective. Leaving the activity fairly open to start with, it developed into a game with much discussion between the children.

The way it worked was that one pair of children would decide what the pot would do to anything that was put into it - this could be a number or a shape. They would give one example, say, *60 goes in, 10 comes out.* The other children then guess what the pot's function is, say, *might it subtract 50* or *divide by 6?* Then they could throw in another number and be told what would come out.

I think the possibilities for this activity are many and within the capabilities of all. I originally used the idea with 7 - 9 year olds and intend using it again with my class of 9 - 10 year olds who have a wide range of mathematical ability.

I would like to hear from anyone else who tries this idea to learn of other applications of it for mathematics and perhaps in other subject areas.

Sue Saunders teaches at Balfour Junior School, Brighton

"But, my dear little wife, I did not take two hats. I haven't got two hats in the world."

"Then how is it that there are two hats in the pot?" asked his wife.

"I know no more than you do," said Mr. Goodbody. "I know I only put one in."

"In that case," said Mrs. Goodbody, "this must be a magic pot, my dear husband, if it can make two hats out of one. Let's see if it can do it again."

She took the hats out of the pot and then she put one of them back. There, sure enough, were two hats, both exactly alike.

"Well," she said, "I was right of course. It is a magic pot. I am going to see if it does it every time."

Sure enough, each time she put a hat in the pot, there was another one beside it, until very soon the room was full of hats, all exactly alike.

"But my dear," said her husband. "What is the good of so many hats? I have only one

head you know."

At this Mrs. Goodbody stopped.

"Yes, I suppose you are right. They are not much use to us. What a pity, and I thought we had got such a useful pot."

"Perhaps," said her husband, "the pot can make other things besides hats. Let us try. Now, what can we put into it?"

"Let's try this bag of flour," said his wife. "It would be very useful to have plenty of flour in the house. There, in it goes."

Mathematics is something young children can talk about. **Jean Edwards** explains how.

A WILD THING

Introduction and background

In September 1991 I attended a maths co-ordinators' course at Knuston run by John Hibbs. One of the activities we took part in was designed to encourage precise mathematical discussion and group co-operation. This activity relied upon our ability, as adults, to read and to perform mathematical calculations.

I wanted to take up this idea with my class, as they would benefit greatly from developing their mathematical vocabulary and being able to use it in many different contexts. My class are a mixture of Y2 and Y3; many of them are fluent Bengali speakers who are learning English as a second language. I wanted to develop the activity so that it could be used in mixed ability groups. A large proportion of the children I teach are pre-readers and so I did not want reading skills to loom large in the activity.

Design of materials

I decided to concentrate on mathematical language related to colour, shape, pattern and position. I also decided to use pictures and parts of pictures. The idea was to have a set of cards; each card would contain a piece of information about a picture. When the group put all these pieces of information together the result would be a finished picture.

I made a set of cards which would result in a clown, a set which would result in a monster, a set which would lead to a wild thing and a set which would lead to a house. The children would have about twenty cards between them. Each card would have a small part of the overall picture and would make no sense unless it was related to all the other cards.

The children would also know generally what their picture would be.

Working with the children

When I first introduced this activity to my class I organised groups to do it with an adult overseeing the work. The adult did not control the activity, but took part and encouraged the children to take turns and listen to each other. When all the children had taken part once with an adult they went on to work on their own in groups.

The only 'rules' we insisted upon were that every child in the group must have a turn at drawing and that whoever was drawing could not draw from their own card but had to be having someone else's card described to them. Nobody was allowed to look at anyone else's card.

The children enjoyed the activity very much, communicating with each other excitedly and loudly. Each group was mixed, and contained children who spoke only English and children who spoke both English and Bengali. In the groups the children used both languages and helped each other with the appropriate word when they knew what to say in Bengali but weren't quite sure in English.

From time to time the children had disputes about taking turns and organising the talking, and they found that listening and taking turns was the only way to work on the activity successfully. I kept all the completed pictures so that groups who had finished could see what other children had made of the same clues. I found that the children could do a set of cards more than once after a certain amount of time and with a different set of children, so that they were talking about different aspects of the picture.

Further developments

The activity was so enjoyable and valuable that I intend to develop it further, with more sets of cards. I shared the idea with the teacher next door and she made a set which required the children to use the correct vocabulary for the parts of the face, as we were doing a lot of work based on the parts of the body at the time.

I also asked the children how they thought the activity could be developed. They were very keen to devise a set of cards to result in a three-dimensional model, possibly using Lego, but as yet I have not decided how we could represent this on two-dimensional cards. As the year goes on and the children's reading skills develop, I would like to try sets of cards, similar to those we used at Knuston, that involve reading.

At a staff seminar I used the adult sets of cards and then the picture cards to share the ideas with the rest of the school. We found that when the teachers used the picture cards the results of their drawing were quite similar to those of the children, in spite of the fact that they were much more precise about their descriptions than the children are as yet.

When I designed the cards I did not do an ultimate finished 'answer', and so all the results the groups achieved were acceptable. But possibly, as the children become more experienced in precise descriptions, their results will get more and more accurate.

Some relevant vocabulary

Colour - red, blue, yellow, green, brown, purple, orange, black, grey.
Simplifications - use a limited number of colours.
Extension - use shades of colours, dark and pale colours.

Shape - circle, square, triangle, rectangle.
Simplifications - use fewer shapes.
Extensions - use more nameable shapes such as pentagon, hexagon; use irregular versions of shapes such as different types of triangles, use irregular shapes which do not have names requiring precise description using terms like bumpy, curved, straight.

Position - top, bottom, left, right, side, under, over, next to, inside, outside, near, and many combinations of the above.
Simplifications - use fewer of these, just the ones being worked on.
Extensions - use these in more combinations and include in front of, behind, in three-dimensional examples. Include distances and sizes in relation to each other.

Other ideas

- Use the vocabulary from whatever topic you are using eg parts of the body, animals, buildings, food.
- Use Lego or building bricks to result in a threedimensional model.
- Use the children themselves so that they end up in various positions, holding different things.
- End up with a pattern, not a picture.

Jean Edwards teaches at Military Road Lower School in Northampton

The wild thing *below* was produced by a group of children, using these cards.
The actual cards are bigger and in colour.
Each child had a few cards. The children took turns, describing each card to another child who added the detail depicted on this card to the group's picture.

Joe Powderly took some Year 5 children on a mathematical quest.

THE QUEST FOR THE 5 DIGIT 6174

I'm language co-ordinator in a junior school. Let me make this clear from the start. The early years of my 'teaching' maths were Hesse, Hesse and more Hesse (and I thought myself then an imaginative teacher!) The beauty of maths had slipped me by. That state of affairs remained I suppose until I read my first Martin Gardner. Or was it Jean, our maths co-ordinator? Or was it SMILE or ATM or the Manchester maths group? I suppose and could still be wrong. However, if there is a moment, I remember a spring Sunday afternoon sitting at my desk, looking out occasionally into a garden of budding flowers and trees, whose names eluded me and reading Brissenden's book on talk in maths. This and Martin Hughes' work invited me into a field from which I once thought I was excluded. My mind was excited by something new.

Into a year 5 classroom in October. The children had been exploring patterns. Take two digits and use them to make 2 numbers Subtract one from the other. The children had discovered that the answers were multiples of 9. And more.

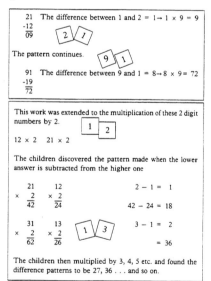

But why stop at 2 digits? 3 digit numbers were subtracted and the children noted the significance of the H and U digits.

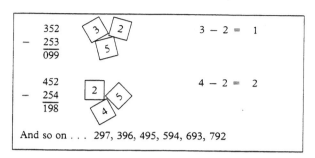

And then to four....

6174

I had read Marilyn Davis' book *"I hate maths!"* and realised that if the answer of a 4-digit calculation is rearranged so that the lower number is subtracted from the higher one, eventually, 6174 will be reached.

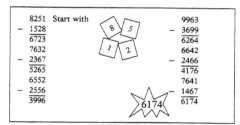

The children were amazed by such a discovery. They tried to prove it wrong. And yet 6174 would always turn up.

So by and by, we had come to 5. But let Faye and Rachel be your guide!!

Faye: You start off with a number and you put the highest number first, then you swop it around. And.. . you keep on doing it until it comes to 6174.

What do you mean, keep on doing it?

Rachel: Sort of keep on. You choose a number and you swap it round. And the answer... You put the highest to the lowest. And you swap it round the lowest to the highest. You keep on doing it until you get to 6174

So you can be doing it for 20, 30 sums.

R: Well!

F: If you keep on going past 6174, then-em!-you'll come out straightaway, because you'll go on and then there will be another 6174. Next sum, 6174.

But how many times will you keep on doing it?

R: It could be ages. Or it could be one sum.

F: It could be a long time.

R: How many sums is a long time?

R: About 20 or so.

F: Yeh

Go on. What do you think will happen with 5 digit numbers?

R: We think it's going to work.

Why?

F: Because 6174 worked. So why not a 5 digit number?

R: Yeh.

You said 4 digits worked. If 6174 works, why will 5 work?

R: I think it will work.

That's what Faye said. Faye said it works for four. Therefore it must work for five.

R & F: That's right. Yeh!

If that's right, does the same thing work with 2 and 3 digits?

F: No!

R (very hesitant): No. Could do. It depends.

Then what is the pattern for 2 and 3 digits?

R: I don't think it will work with 2 digits, but it could work with 3.

Is there a pattern with 2 and 3 digits?

R: Don't know. I never tried it!

(exasperated): Yes you have! You have done loads of sums with 2 and 3 digits, Rachel.

R: I don't remember.

The first thing you did was 2 and 3 digits. (Shows Rachel her old work).

R: Oh this!

Yes

F & R: It's all in the 9 times table.

OK?

F: In my maths book, it always equal. Like 72 .. 99.

There's a pattern for 2 and 3 digits? If Faye says there's a pattern for four, there must be a pattern for five. So is there a pattern for 2 and 3? That's all I am asking.

R: Yeh, 9 times table.

Something to do with the 9 times table. Is that all?

R: Yeh (pauses). I don't think it's going to work with a 10 digit number. It might work with 5.

You say it's going to work with 5. How are you going to do it?

R: Choose a number.

F: And go on. If you kind of, sort of get the same number, everytime.

A March morning

The children are using calculators in search of the 5 digit 6174 within a two-hour

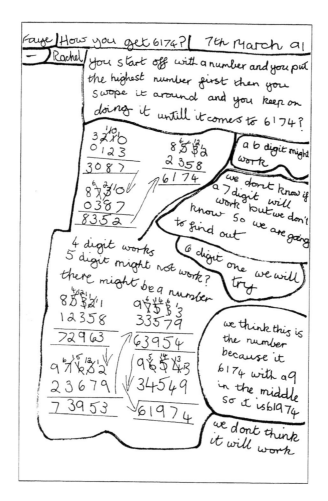

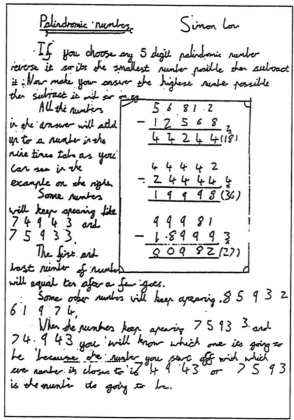

lesson. (Some children have already chosen to work on this activity previously.)
Rachel, in her remarks, is shown to be hesitant.

'No it could do. Depends.' She can make an arbitrary statement like, 'I don't think it will work with 2 digits, but it could work with 3', after investigating 2 and 3 digit numbers in October. However, she first of all states that she had never done the work. 'Don't know. I never tried it.' And when challenged, admits that she cannot remember.

However, she can remember and follow the steps required to find 6174. She knows as well that this series could take a long time. 'It could be ages or it could be one sum.' She can see it's something to do with the 9 times table. 'It's all in the 9 times table.' 'Yeh. 9 times table.'

Faye says less than Rachel. She misses out bits, when trying to narrate the steps needed to make 6174. She warns of the pitfalls in continuing after reaching 6174. 'You'll come out straightaway, because you'll go on and then there will be another 6174.' She understands it's something to do with the 9 times table and gives examples. She also gives an indicator of success in their search. 'If you kind of, sort of, get the same number, everytime.'
Faye, like Rachel, is operating in an intuitive way, but working towards judgements based on some selective evidence.

As Faye says, 'because 6174 works. So why not a 5 digit number?'

Why not? But how is this model used?

The written work

Faye and Rachel explain how 6174 works.
*   they then speculate about 6 and 7 digit numbers, as well as 4 and 5
*   they give one example of what they find out
*   they make a generalisation, based on one finding and an observation of the number 6174

*   they then contradict themselves. 'We don't think it will work.'

Faye and Rachel did more than one example. At least, ten. Were they rigging the results? Were they trying to give their evidence order?

Let's continue the quest with Simon. Let him speak.

Simon: We're doing maths with 4 and 5 digits. We're also doing work with 2 and 3 digits. On the 2, there is a pattern. If you take . . . all the answers are in the 9 times table. When you get a 2 digit number and reverse it. So when you reverse it, it will be in the 9 times table. We know what it is by taking the 2 numbers away like 7 and 1, for example, seven take away 1 is 6 50 the answer will be 54 (6 times 9). For the 3-digit number, there's also a pattern. It's to do with the difference between the first and last number.

With 5 digit numbers. I haven't quite found the number, but I'm trying it now.

What about 4 digit numbers?

The 4 digit number. Eh. Everytime, you choose a 4 digit number, then you swap it round to make the smallest number you can get. You take it away. Then you keep on doing it until you get 6174.

What about the first number? The number you have to take away from? What's special about that number?

It's the 9 times table?

Possibly (pauses).

When you get your answer, what must you do with it?

You must make it the highest number.

(repeats what Simon has just said): *Do you think it's going to work?*

Maybe.

How long have you been working on this?

For quite a long time.

In hours. 10..? 2..? How long have you been working on this. Roughly. How many hours has it felt like? (Teacher jokes) *A very long time. How many hours?*

Since I actually started?

Yes.

About 5.

You say about 5. And have you got a number?

Well. I got a few numbers, but they keep changing all the time.

Well what are you going to do? What are these few numbers?

There's 74943, 73953, 61974. Some other numbers, I can't remember.

When you started, did you think you could find a number?

Yeh.

Now after 5 hours, what do you think?

It might work.

(Repeats): *Do you think it's because it's very difficult or it's the way you're going about doing it or the number doesn't exist?*

I think the number does exist, but it keeps changing.

So you think it's numbers. How many numbers do you think it might be?

Well about 5.

Quite a lot of numbers. Instead of one, you think it's 5. Well, find the five numbers.

They keep on appearing.

It is obvious that Simon is further on in the quest. He explains clearly the pattern made by the subtraction of 2 and 3 digit numbers. He has to be reminded about 4 digit numbers and forgets that the answer has to be rearranged to make the highest number.

He is faced with conflicting evidence. He thinks he has found an answer, but with additional evidence, he finds new possibilities. When talking to me, he mentions 74943, 73953 and 61974. In his written report, 85932 and 75933 now appear and 73953 is discounted or forgotten. As he says 'I thing the number exists, but it keeps changing.'

Simon had been working for 5 hours - on three occasions - to try and crack the 5 digit 6174.

He had been given a successful model, which had worked in one circumstance, but now had to try to use this in similar circumstances. The more he worked, the more he became uncertain. Simon says, 'well I got a few numbers, but they keep on changing.'

He seeks one number, but he has found at least five and that's where I'll leave it for the time being, though the children's quest continues.

We are entering the outer portals of Chaos Theory. When I was reading James Gleick's *'Chaos'* I was struck by the way scientists played for days and days on computers to unravel apparently random numbers and find some kind of 'order', for example Robert May's work on fish populations and Benoit Mandelbrot's early work on cotton prices.

In his own way, Simon grappling with the figures,' of 74943, 73953, 61974, 85932 and 75933 on the display of a Casio pocket calculator, is trying to find order and pattern.

Joe Powderly teaches in Surbiton, Surrey

Naomi Wells kept quiet, so that her pupils could ask the questions.

NINETY-NINE

I am currently attending a twenty day mathematics course, which is spread over a period of time. One of our tasks was to set up an investigation based on the answer to a question being 99.

I teach year six, and had done so for several years, and so I was interested to see what the pupils' reaction would be. I therefore planned for the investigation to be as open-ended as possible and hoped not to put any bias or restriction on ideas by suggesting my own, or by giving examples. This was the hardest part of the task, me keeping quiet!

I was team teaching and the other members of staff were happy for me to lead the activity across two classes of mixed ability year six: fifty-four children in all. We have a large open area in our purpose-built middle school, so I arranged for two strips of wallpaper, about seven metres each in length, to be laid out on the floor with a quantity of felt tip pens.

In the classroom the children were asked to write in their notebooks, without any discussion, a possible question if the answer was 99. I said nothing else, and just waited.

Very soon all the children had several questions written, including a wide variety of ideas.
They chose one of their questions to write on the long wallpaper stretch. They had to show their question to a member of staff, just so that they didn't alter it when they saw other ideas.
We had time to look at the wallpaper stretches, discuss some of the questions or add another from our list.

Some people checked answers, whilst others tried out questions on calculators. As the questions were anonymous the writer could also check their own. Some were corrected, but not crossed out or removed. We continued later in the week with further lessons, keeping the wallpaper for ideas.

The next task I set was to follow an investigation of their own to do with the '99' questions. Individually, in pairs or groups, as long as they could tell me what they were going to investigate, they would be allowed to do it. Some chose possible additions, or subtractions, others went on to combinations, and some were on worded questions.

One group chose to investigate which two even numbers added to get 99[!] When they realised the impossibility of their task, they were a little despondent until I pointed out how much they had learnt by their mistake.

Robert asked if he could have a piece of wallpaper to himself. He was not usually one to work on his own, although capable of doing so. I asked why. He explained he wanted to make the longest question that he could. I gave him the wallpaper. A few days later he had half covered the paper. I asked if he was working it out as he went along. "No," came the reply, "when I get to the bottom line I will check the answer so far and do something to it to get it back to 99." I was impressed, but had to point out that he had already reached 99 in the top line. "Oh dear, never mind, I'll start again," came the reply. He did, completing lines at home, at school and in the dinner hour.

Finally, Robert reached the bottom line of his paper, worked out the total that far and continued with 1/2 + 7/14 - 4/2 divided by 6 - 23 2/4 + 1/2 - 8/16 + 1/4 - 2.75 divided by 10 - 0.5 multiplied by 3 multiplied by 3 divided by 4 - 1/2 - 2/8 + 50/100 divided by 4 multiplied by 56 divided by 8 + 1 divided by 6 multiplied by 12 + 30 - 40/20 - 1 = 99 [!]

Meanwhile Carina had come to ask, "Can we really investigate *anything*?" "Yes" I confirmed. "In that case" she replied, "can I investigate Robert? I want to know where he gets his ideas from."

She then set about trying to find out how Robert and others got their ideas. Her heading read:

An investigation to see how people get their ideas.

In another corner I spotted the heading CODED LETTERS. I went to investigate. Dean and Matthew explained that they had worked out a code. As they were on about the seventh line of A + A + A + A + A + A + A. I asked "Does A = 1" "Yes, how did you know?" they asked.

We continued the conversation with me asking how many A's they would have to write '99' came the answer. I asked them to think if there was a quicker way of writing this, and when I returned a little later they had put,

After a discussion we decided to do it this way
A   99 times
B   49 times + A
C   33 times
D   24 times + A
E   19 times + A
... they continued down to ...
I   11 times.

There were some errors, but at this point I didn't think that mattered.

A great deal of number work, discussion, examining and re-examining of ideas continued. We could easily have continued this investigation for several weeks. I told the children that I was going to keep their work to show some other teachers, so did not display it.

Two months later, as the summer holiday came in between, I told the same class that I would be away as I was going to my maths course.

"Are you taking our 99 work?" they asked. Obviously a memorable task, which all abilities had found very challenging, and I had a wonderful time teaching.

On reflection, what have I learnt?

It is very easy to stand back and know that those children had a positive learning experience and environment. That they developed their concept of number and algebra. They were able to plan and develop an investigation and learn from their results.

But what did *I* learn?

- I can leave the children to decide on the materials they need and how to go about something.
- I can give them something very open to work with and not limit the results.
- I can give them a question without it having a specific answer.
- I can keep control of my classroom when they are all over the place doing all sorts of things!
- I should be doing this more often, as it gave me greater freedom to understand their capabilities, to help them with their difficulties, and to provide them with a situation in which they could learn.

In *Thinking Things Through* [1984] Leone Burton wrote 'The greatest value of this approach is in the effect it has on the classroom. Hesitancy and dependency in pupils are replaced by confidence and autonomy.' I'm inclined to agree.

Naomi Wells teaches at College Heath Middle School, Mildenhall, Suffolk.

Other Useful Publications for the Primary Classroom from the ATM

Starting Points/Activity Books

Primary Points of Departure, a collection of more than 70 starting points covering many aspects of the National Curriculum for KS 2.

Exploring Mathematics with Younger Children. A collection of starting points and investigations suitable for young children. KS1

Mathematical Activities from Poland. Activities using dice, dominoes, cubes, coins. KS2

The What, Why How and When of Mathematics Trails, gives practical advice on running a maths trail.

10^2 Book and Poster. Full of ideas and investigations based on the 10 by 10 number square. KS2

Squares, Patterns and Quilts. Useful when looking at shape and space, and also cross curricular work.

P'raps, P'raps Not. Originally designed as a resource for younger children for covering probability, but still a useful book when covering Data Handling.

Polygon Dot to Dot. A Photocopyable resource. The masters are ideal when looking at shape and exploring reflective and rotational symmetry

Transforming. An activity book where the role of ICT is emphasised.

Card and Posters

Tiling Pattern Postcards. 16 full colour cards of paving stone patterns. Ideal for showing children how symmetry and tessellation are part of their world.

Holes Activity Pack. 16 colour cards showing holes as seen in the environment, as well as 8 computer generated images and a booklet of ideas

Polyhedra Postcards. Eight full colour cards showing a total of 34 Polyhedra. They are ideal to help children become familiar with 3D shape names.

Out and About Postcards. 16 colour cards taken 'out and about' which can lead to discussion about pattern, shape and much more! Includes book of teachers notes.

Number Posters. Set of Posters that cover various aspects of Number and Numeracy.

Practical Resources

Mathematical Activity Tiles. Polygon dripmats (MATs) are ideal for investigating shape and space, tessellations, reflection, rotation, angle and tiling patterns. Ideal for both 2D and 3D work. MATs are available in the following shapes:

Triangles, Squares, Pentagons, Hexagons, Octagons, Isosceles Triangles, Rectangles, Decagons, and Dodecagons

Tiling Generators. Thick cardboard squares (2 designs) and hexagons (5 designs) all match when used together. Children can make an endless variety of patterns. They are ideal for mathematical investigations and artistic creations and work connected with shape, space, angles, transformations and patterns.

A book accompanies the tiles.

All the above publications can be found in the ATM Publications Catalogue, available from the ATM office.

ATM, 7 Shaftesbury Street,
Derby, DE23 8YB
Telephone 01332 346599

ERC

455011 – Extension 4009